CHRISTIANITY IN

THE COMPUTER AGE

CHRISTIANITY IN THE COMPUTER AGE

by

A. Q. MORTON AND JAMES McLEMAN

HARPER & ROW, PUBLISHERS

New York and Evanston

CONTENTS

5

The authors of this book are engaged on a more technical study of the letters of Paul and their importance for our knowledge of the origins of the Christian Faith. The investigation was carried out using an electric computer and the results will be of more interest to the biblical scholar than to the average person.

This work on the Pauline Epistles, however, has raised some issues which are important to all Christians. The publishers have therefore asked us to write a simple and non-technical explanation of the work which has been done and to give our own views on the wider issues which arise from it.

This present book therefore expresses a contemporary view of the Bible, the church and personal religion.

James McLeman,
The Manse,
BURGHEAD,
Moray.

A. Q. Morton,
The Abbey Manse,
CULROSS,
Fife.

On the Bible Today

To many people the Bible is a book to be read and to be revered. The idea of reading the Bible in a critical spirit never occurs to them, not because they are afraid of the results of any critical inquiry, but just because they know that the critical reading of any great literature tends to build a barrier between the reader and the book. The man who reads the latest Shakespearian scholar's account of the origins of *King Lear* must often feel that the scholar has missed the finest features of the play and spent all his time and energy on trivial details. He does not intend to let this happen to his reading of the Bible.

To many people the Bible is the most important book of all; it is the word of God. Asked to explain this phrase, different people would give different reasons for its use, but all the answers would include the same ingredients in various mixtures. The Bible is a book about God; about the dealings between God and men: it has been shown, by long experience, to be, in itself, a unique instrument of communication between God and man. In the Bible you read about God, about men and women of all times and of all conditions and how God has dealt with them; you may find in the Bible a counterpart to some experience of your own so that God will seem to speak to you from the pages of this book. To many, wandering in the wilderness or sitting out the dark night in the garden of Gethsemane are not stories in an old book but vivid descriptions of parts of their own life.

Why then, you might ask, try to persuade people to risk this heritage and start reading the Bible critically? The only answer is necessity. There are three reasons why you must read the Bible critically.

The first reason is that individual reading and interpretation – and this must include churches and organisations as well as isolated men and women – result in conflicting and absurd interpretations of the Bible.

Not much over a hundred years ago people in Scotland were burned for being witches. In the atmosphere of the age it was not an unreasonable construction of the evidence. People were so afraid of witches that, if they had a spell put on them, they would die. So putting a spell on someone was indirect murder. In time people came to their senses and recovered their courage and stopped believing in witches, and as they ceased to believe in witches they stopped killing them. An important element in the situation had been the biblical passages which showed that witches had existed in Israel, had been detected and had been killed. A text which illustrated an ancient illusion had been used to foster a new one.

The days of dangerous and eccentric interpretation are not ended. There are sects in Scotland, at the present time, who will not allow any of their members to share a meal with any person, even their wife or husband, who does not share their view of the Bible. The text on which this nonsense is based, in the name of Christianity, is "be not unequally yoked with unbelievers". This is understood to command complete separation from the rest of mankind who are not in the fellowship of the saints. No member of the sect can run a grocer's shop, for he would have to sell goods to unbelievers. An interesting exception is that members can teach people to drive motor cars, for this new occupation has not been mentioned in the Bible.

These are two simple illustrations of the fact that texts from the Bible have been used to justify eccentricities, crimes and excesses without number. As soon as you try to discover what the text meant in its original setting, and deduce the legitimate modern application, you have begun to read the Bible critically.

The second reason for reading the Bible critically is that it was written critically. A simple impression of the Bible is that everything in the Bible happened in an orderly, if rather convoluted, sequence. Moses met God beside a burning bush, went back to his people who were in bondage, led them out, after some dramatic interludes, and took them to the border of the promised land.

But all this was written down long after the events happened and the writer can see how the winner ran the race with rare judgement. Actually Moses must have had great difficulty in convincing the people of his ability, sincerity and authority. In his old age they were not any more willing to accept him than they had been in his youth.

The retrospective view, found in every book of the Bible, except possibly Revelation, colours the picture in every part. Isaiah is a great man to us; in his own day he was challenged and opposed. Paul is now accepted as a religious genius but Peter thought him a mis-leader of the early church.

Reading the Bible critically, therefore, is to treat it as a living book. When Peter says yea and Paul says nay, it only makes sense when you see the two men struggling to discover the truth. A living man, fighting to get his views accepted and, like every man who ever lived, having errors of fact and judgement mixed in with his truths, has more to say to us than any cardboard cut-out of a flawless saint.

Hence, to read the Bible critically is to read it as it was written.

The third reason for reading the Bible critically is that to do so is inescapable in a scientific age. No longer is there any honourable intellectual alternative.

Writing about A.D. 40, the prominent Jewish scholar Philo compiled a commentary on Genesis. He could not accept the view that the world had been made in seven days. Philo calls the creation story in Genesis a "myth" and puts forward his view that a day is not a day but a period of time. Since then the fundamental difficulty of relating statements in the Bible to the knowledge of secular science has much increased.

To take an obvious example: when Jesus lived and the

11

Gospels were written, people had no idea equivalent to our modern idea of a miracle. That age had no conception of laws or regularity in nature. To us a miracle is impossible: by definition it is something which could not happen. To them there was no line to be drawn between the exceptional and the impossible.

*   *   *

So whether we like it or not, we all live in a world in which some of the primary statements of the Bible – that people rose from the dead or turned water into wine or multiplied food four thousandfold – are no longer credible. The main question of our times, and it is only an old question much sharpened by circumstances, is simply, "Is the Bible true?"

In connection with the Bible the word "truth" is often used in two different senses. This need cause no trouble if the two senses are always distinguished. Not only do they sometimes become confused by accident, however, but a frequent resource of the theologian is to try and change from one meaning to the other as an escape from some logical dilemma.

Most often when we ask if a story is true we are merely asking if it is historically verifiable and credible. Mark tells the dramatic story of how John the Baptist was beheaded. When we ask if this story is true or false we can make a list of the historical statements it contains and check them against the records of the times. What is of interest in this example is that almost every factual statement in the story is wrong. The names of the people are hopelessly confused. So you must conclude that, in this historical sense, the story is not true.

However, a lesson can be drawn from the story. We all know that a feature of protracted sensual indulgence is the destruction of judgement so that exaggerated responses such as rash wagers, foolish promises and ridiculous boasts are often made. So this story can be used as a valid comment on human nature, used to teach a general truth about humanity, and in this sense it is true.

In the beheading of John the Baptist the contrast between the two types of truth, the literal, factual, historic truths and the symbolic, illustrative, literary truths, is clear. But what of a story like the raising of Lazarus as told in the eleventh chapter of the Gospel of John?

There was, and is, now a place called Bethany. Like enough a man called Lazarus lived there in the days of Jesus. But was a man raised from the dead in this way, in that place, at that time? Putting the question in this way telescopes two questions. These are better considered separately. The first is, What did the man who wrote the story mean to say? and then, Must we accept what the author would have us believe?

On a first encounter the story of the raising of Lazarus reads like a simple historical narrative. But the author of the fourth Gospel is fond of allegory and symbolism. If you read the story over a second time and compare it with the resurrection of Jesus as recounted later in the same book, you can hardly fail to notice that every detail in the one story is matched by a contrasting detail in the other. Lazarus comes forth with difficulty; Jesus rises effortlessly and silently. Lazarus bursts his bands; Jesus leaves them neatly folded.

Soon it is impossible to suppress the thought that this story may not be a historical narrative at all but a deliberate contrast to the resurrection of Jesus inserted to throw the later story into bold relief. At this point it becomes relevant that this incident, so central to this Gospel, is unknown to the authors of the other three Gospels.

Of course, you can avoid the embarrassing series of coincidences in this story of the raising of Lazarus by taking the view that it is a purely symbolic story, not true in the historical sense but true in the psychological sense. But this will leave you facing a nasty problem. Someone will then have put words into the mouth of Jesus which He may not have spoken. And if this is so, or even possibly so, in one case, then all the other sayings of Jesus must be looked at too.

The position can be summed up thus. Many of the Bible stories are now incredible. They cannot have happened as they are set down. Sometimes the difficulties are historical–difficulties of places, people and dates–but in other cases the difficulties are philosophical or scientific. We may reject a story not because of any statement it makes but because the story runs counter to our modern knowledge. It must be admitted that not everything is known yet, but we can only act and judge on what we do know. It might be that some succeeding generation will find the raising of Lazarus to be true for them in a sense in which it cannot be true for us.

In the Bible the most difficult problems are set by the stories which may have had a historical foundation, but have been so modified for didactic reasons that one can no longer be sure either of the history or the moral purpose which has reshaped the narratives. One such incident is the turning of the water into wine, where one man can extract a moral but another will regretfully confess his complete bewilderment.

All of this means that the Bible cannot be read or accepted uncritically. The typical figure of the evangelist, clutching his Bible to his breast and thundering "The Bible says!" is not speaking with divine authority; he is declaring his unwillingness to use, in his religion, the care and thought he exercises when choosing wallpaper or cashing a cheque.

There are people who have always read the Bible uncritically and will continue to do so. Their own life and experience has been made rich by the recorded experience of the men and women of the Bible. They can continue to read the Bible uncritically: for the discrimination which the mind should make their heart and life makes for them. But most of us must use the means of critical assessment which are available to us, or forfeit our integrity.

14

CHAPTER ONE

THE CRITICAL APPROACH TO THE BIBLE

The first rule for the critical study of the Bible is a simple one: read the Bible exactly as you read any other ancient book. You may decide that the Bible is not like any other book, but this must be your conclusion and not your starting point.

The Bible is not one book; it is two collections of books. The first collection, the thirty-nine books from Genesis to Malachi, the Old Testament, make up the sacred books of the Jewish religion. The interest of the Old Testament for Christians, though great, is indirect. The Old Testament is the Bible which Jesus knew and it is also a record of religious thought and action from the Stone Age up to a few centuries before the time of Jesus.

Appreciation of the Old Testament is made difficult by a number of factors. An obvious one is that the books are not in order of age; Genesis, which not only stands first in the collection but deals with the creation of the universe, is one of the later books. Some of the books, Joshua and Judges for example, which come after it, are older books in their present form.

Again, many of the Old Testament books show clear traces of having been revised to suit the ideas of later ages. Stories and traditions are duplicated and modified as, for instance, in the two accounts of the creation, the flood and the crossing of the Red Sea. Another obvious difficulty is that Hebrew is a simple language, with a small vocabulary, compared with English and all other modern languages. The same Hebrew word may be translated in half a dozen different ways with as many possible interpretations. There are some Old Testament passages, notably in the book of Psalms and in Isaiah, of which no adequate translation has yet been made.

But the most formidable barrier is the attitude of Christianity to the Old Testament. The customary view is that the Hebrew religion, as shown in the Old Testament, was an early stage in religious development based on an inferior revelation. There is some truth in this contention, but not nearly as much as is commonly claimed or unconsciously assumed. If any Christian doubts this he need only read the Koran in which the books of the New Testament are treated by Muslims as Christians treat the books of the Old Testament.

One result of this superior attitude towards the Old Testament has been that it is read as a tamer and much more respectable book than it really is. In the Old Testament are records of human sacrifice and ritual slaughter, and the ingenious attempts to explain these away have extracted the flavour from the books. An example of this is the action of Abraham who took Isaac up a mountain to sacrifice him. The explanation which is most often offered from the pulpit or the pages of the commentaries is that this was God's way of testing Abraham. The alternative explanation is that after the Israelites had abandoned the sacrifice of their first-born some rationalising explanation was needed to justify the change. The reason was given in this story: I need not sacrifice my child since Abraham did not sacrifice Isaac.

By and large the Old Testament is not difficult to read critically. Once you accept that it is a library extending over 2,000 years of ancient history and stop trying to draw Christian moral lessons from it, you see it for what it is, a priceless record of human nature in action. The folly and grandeur of mankind's perennial search for God are recorded in these thirty-nine books.

In a real sense, all you have to do is stand back and let the Old Testament speak for itself. Its claims are modest, by New Testament standards, and its men and women are recognisably the same as ourselves.

CHAPTER TWO

READING THE NEW TESTAMENT
CRITICALLY

In most Bibles the Old Testament is separated from the New Testament by a single blank leaf. This apparently insignificant gap is in fact quite crucial. Between the Old Testament and the New Testament is a space of about 300 years, and it was in those centuries that the world in which Jesus lived was made. It was in those years that Greek became the common literary language, the language in which the New Testament is written. It was then that the ideas of resurrection and of a future life were conceived. So when you turn the single page from the Old Testament to the New Testament you are passing in time from the world of Shakespeare to the world of Queen Victoria, or from the age of the Pilgrim Fathers to the age of the atom.

*   *   *

The New Testament is a collection of twenty-seven books written by hand – one reason why they are so short – in Greek during the century which began in about A.D. 40. Twenty-one of these books are letters, epistles as they are entitled in the Authorised Version. Some of these, like Philemon, are personal letters such as we write and send today. Others, Hebrews or James for example, were meant for more general use and might be called tracts or pamphlets now. The Corinthian letters were sent, as were some others, not to an individual but to a church.

When you come to the critical study of a letter you want to know who wrote it, to whom it was sent and the reason why it was written and sent. Then, when you have understood just what the letter meant to the writer and to the recipient, you can tell what there is in it that might be relevant to our life in the twentieth century.

Regrettably little is known of the origins of our New Testament letters. It is likely that the twenty-seven books were gathered together about A.D. 150. The oldest copies of the New Testament which are anything like complete date from the fourth century and so are as far from some of the originals as we are from the seventeenth century. Paul disappears from history around A.D. 63, yet the first trace of his letters is A.D. 95 at the earliest, and is more likely to be about A.D. 135.

Sometimes it is possible to tell a great deal from a study of the letter itself. For example, Paul had done much for the Galatians and resented strongly the charge that his teaching lacked authority. He writes them a sharp and angry letter dealing with this subject. But in many cases we can only guess. A Gospel bears the name John; so does Revelation and three letters. But it is unlikely that these are by one and the same John, though this was assumed for a long time. Just think of the problems that would arise for us if only first names were used and surnames were omitted from our correspondence and catalogues.

If you cannot be sure of the identity of the author of an epistle you can only guess at the circumstances in which it was written and the precise significance of the statements in it. There may be lessons in it for the twentieth century, but you will always have the uncomfortable feeling that, if so much is uncertain, these may be uncertain too.

So there is a sense in which the study of an epistle must begin with the questions, Who wrote it? When and where did he write it? To whom was it sent, and why was it written and sent? These questions are not independent of each other, and it is clear that you cannot be sure of answering any of them unless you can confidently answer the first of them.

The six remaining books of the New Testament are the

four Gospels, the book of Acts of the Apostles, and the series of cryptic and symbolic visions rather inappropriately titled the Revelation of John.

The four Gospels deal with the life, work, teaching and death of Jesus. The Acts of the Apostles is the second part of the Gospel of Luke, a fact which is totally obscured by the insertion of the Gospel of John between them. Acts is a journalistic account of that part of the early church which was known to the author.

The book of Revelation seems very strange to us, but this type of book was familiar in the time of Jesus. It is a series of puzzling visions in which the characters all represent some person or party or principle. From the earliest days no one was sure if all that Revelation foretold had happened, or if some had happened and some lay still in the future, or if all the events were yet to come. In many parts Revelation is a sub-Christian book, and it is difficult to see what difference it would make to any of us whichever view of its prophecies prevailed.

These six books – the Gospels, Acts and Revelation – are not composed in the same way as the letters. A man who writes a letter makes it up and sets it down in what is essentially one operation. Even if he dictates his letter the proposition is not changed. What goes down in the letter comes from the mind of its author. With the Gospels the situation is quite different.

Suppose the man writing a Gospel puts down a parable. It was composed by Jesus and not made up by the writer who simply copies reports of men who had been present at events which he did himself not witness. In the case of both Matthew and Luke sections from other books are copied, for it is clear that these two men used passages from the Gospel of Mark. As they copy from the Gospel of Mark the distinctive methods of each of the authors can be seen. It is likely that they shared other sources than the Gospel of Mark, for there are places where the Gospels of Matthew and of Luke agree closely yet are not copying from the Gospel of Mark or from each other.

The Gospels of Mark and of John are likely to have been made up in this way also. They contain reports of incidents at which the writer could not have been present, and, unless his account is to be regarded as a fictional reconstruction of events, he must have relied on the accounts of others for his description.

The Book of Revelation stands alone. It claims to be the product of a trance state, but this view is difficult to maintain because some passages in this book are parallel to passages in other books of this kind. If it could be shown that Revelation has been made up from bits and pieces, the comfortable explanation of all the obscurities, that they reflect the fact it is a vision, cannot survive.

The author of a book like a Gospel is not so much an author in our contemporary sense of the word, as an editor, a man who decides what will go in to a book, who will fit the selected portions together and who will compose only the linking material which will give smoothness to the whole book.

In one way the problem of the composite book and the problem of the epistle is the same. Though the religious value of any of them does not depend on who wrote it or how the pieces came to be put together in the form in which we now have them, your interpretation of many passages in the book must remain speculative to a degree, if you cannot tell how the book was written and by whom.

The simplest example of this is the saying of Jesus about divorce. This is recorded in the Gospel of Mark without qualification: Mark x: 1–12. The Gospel of Matthew v: 32 adds the exception of divorce for adultery. There is no doubt that whatever view you may take of the question it is important to know which account is earlier, and if it could be proved, as some churches have argued, that Matthew is the disciple and close companion of Jesus and wrote all of this book from his own close personal experience, then this information is important.

The effect of a lack of factual information about a book is most clearly seen in the case of Revelation. In scholastic circles this book is regarded as having the least value of all the New Testament books. To the layman, especially the unlearned and unsophisticated, it is the key book in the whole New Testament. To the scholar, a puzzling patchwork; to the believer, a vision from heaven.

Because there are these two different kinds of book in the New Testament, two quite contrasting approaches are needed if you are to learn anything about the origins of the books.

In one sense the problem of the epistle is simpler and can be looked at first. It may surprise many people to find there is a problem, for most of the epistles open with an introduction in which the writer clearly identifies himself and often sends greetings to the recipient of the epistle. Unfortunately this is rarely to be trusted and then only after examination. There are two reasons why this should be so.

The first motive for forgery is financial. Not long after the speech-writer Isocrates had died, his own son is complaining that the booksellers have been putting his father's name on any rubbish. With such a name they can sell stuff which otherwise would lie on their shelves. The point of interest in this example is that Isocrates' own son was not sure exactly what his father had written and in one respect, namely the forensic speeches, was mistaken. So you must be on guard against the imposition of merchants.

The second motive was that of authority, in its meaning of prestige and reputation. If you had some views and wrote a book, little attention might be paid to them, but if you put the name of some great authority at the head, it would receive attention. There are many books in the names of Moses and Plato and Aristotle which cannot conceivably have had any connection with the men whose names they bear. A common practice, which is relevant to the New Testament, is for the head or leader of some institution to have his name put on all the books written by his colleagues, students or disciples. A clear case of this is to be seen with the physician Hippocrates. There are more than seventy books which bear his name. Some are by him, some may be research work directed by him, some are by his students and were the product of his school, and some are envious imitations trying to cash in on the reputation of the great Hippocrates. Sorting these works out into the genuine books by Hippocrates, those which if not by him have some connection with him, and those which are completely spurious is not easy.

So the position is that for the works of any Greek writer the ascriptions at the start and end of a book are never to be accepted without supporting evidence, and if any work is full of clear statements about the identity of its author these are likely to be evidence of its dubiety. It is not Paul but his imitators who have to repeat that this is Paul writing.

The great difficulty about the New Testament epistles, and the fourteen epistles from Romans to Hebrews which have been coupled with the name of Paul in particular, is that they appear in the clear light of history only about A.D. 135. For seventy years they lie hidden from our view. So what we have as traditions about their authorship is what people thought in the middle of the second century. With no really reliable evidence from history or tradition to guide us, the only way to discover who wrote these epistles is to study the epistles themselves. This is what scholars have been doing for centuries.

The difficulty about deciding who wrote letters from a study of the letters themselves, is an obvious one; the pattern of argument is circular.

Suppose two scholars sit down to study a group of epistles. They might select one as being universally accepted as the work of the particular author, and contrast with this another which both scholars agree to show considerable differences from the first. They will agree on what the differences are and draw up a complete list of where they are to be seen. Then the two scholars will come to exactly the opposite conclusion and try to support their argument with the same evidence. One scholar will say that all these differences show the two contrasting moods of the same man and go on to describe the circumstances which produced the moods. The other scholar will say that the differences demand the existence of two authors and show how the men can be distinguished. These scholars are not being foolish, they are struggling with an argument which cannot solve their problem. If you question both of them you will get the same answers:

Question – How do you know this man's letters?

Answer – I see his mind and style in them.

Question – How do you recognise his mind and style?

Answer – I see them in his letters.

To escape from this dilemma you must do two things. The first is to set aside the particular problem you may be interested in and examine the class to which your problem belongs. In the case of the Pauline letters you are to look at all writers of Greek prose who are setting down what they themselves have made up. For if you really have discovered a method which will determine the authorship of Paul's letter you should be able to do as much for the letters of Plato, or Isocrates or Demosthenes.

The second step you must take is to devise a general analytical system which can be used on all these Greek authors. Inevitably this will be a numerical system based on the calculation of probability. Your aim is to discover what habits are shared by all writers of Greek prose but are expressed by each writer in his own individual variation. Such a habit will be found in all his genuine writings in a consistent pattern and any spurious works will be likely to show a different pattern. The guarantee that you are not misled by a change of subject matter or by the interval of twenty years is that you can examine these patterns in other writers where these circumstances apply and the pattern is not affected in this way. The patterns in which you are interested are those which are changed beyond the accepted limits by differences in authorship.

A SCIENTIFIC APPROACH

There is no magical solution to this problem. It requires observation and experiment, though the nature of the problem offers some clues for success. If the test is to be a habit, it must be something simple. If you want to be able to make any useful judgement about Greek prose you must be able to do something with around 100 sentences. For example, Demosthenes has sixty-one works to his name. One-third are less than 100 sentences, and all his epistles are less than 100; one-third lie between 100 and 200 sentences; and one-third are more than 200 sentences in length. If your test needed a thousand sentences to be useful it would hardly be practical. In fact you need to look at things which you will find, on the average, on any page of Greek prose.

The first suggestion that tests of this kind could be devised was made by Augustus De Morgan writing in 1859 when he was Professor of Mathematics in University College, London. De Morgan began by observing that some people are addicted to long words. So he argued that, if you counted the number of letters in each word and so worked out the average size of the words used by authors, this would distinguish one from another. The man who chose long words would have a higher average word-length than his colleague who preferred the short words. The actual example used by De Morgan as an illustration was the epistle to the Hebrews.

Unfortunately this test is not of much practical value. The words we write depend to a large extent on the subject matter, and so the samples show, not differences between authors, but differences in subject matter. It might be possible to use word length as a test of authorship by taking samples from a wide range of subjects all by the author under examination, but such samples would be large, certainly too large to be of much interest in Biblical scholarship.

The first tests of word length seem to have been made in 1896 and 1901 by Thomas Corwin Mendenhall. He looked at the Shakespeare–Bacon problem and was able to show by using samples of several hundred thousand words of English, that the Baconian authorship is hardly to be regarded as a serious hypothesis.

The next advance was made by Udny Yule, the Professor of Mathematics in Cambridge, just before the second world war, and his work is described in his pioneer volume, *The Study of Literary Vocabulary*. Udny Yule looked at a number of possible indicators of authorship. One of these was sentence length. Every word we use is part of a sentence, and so the test is comprehensive. We write sentences from one word up to more than 200, so the test is sensitive. Yule looked at sentence length in English authors by counting the number of words in samples of some hundreds of successive sentences in prose writers.

It was not Yule who made sentence length into a reliable tool but Dr. W. C. Wake. The particular problem Wake selected for investigation was one already mentioned, the collection of over seventy works coupled with the name of Hippocrates. Among other tests Wake looked at sentence length distributions in a number of Greek authors.

The mathematical principles of an argument of this type are very simple, but there are many people to whom simple mathematical arguments are anything but obvious. Think of two nations. The average height of men in one, say the French, is 5 ft. 8 in., in the other, say the British, 5 ft. 10 in. Obviously you can tell nothing about the nationality of any one man, for he might be any height from 4 ft. up to 7 ft., or if you have one man of 5 ft. 9 in. you cannot tell if he is a tall Frenchman or a short Briton. To make any judgement about the nationality of men you need a number of men, a number which enables you to include some representatives of all the heights you find in the nations. You must be careful in selecting your men, for if you took all the owners of Rolls-Royces you might find that they were better fed than most people and so were taller. A truly reliable sampling system gives every member of the population an equal chance of being chosen for the sample.

If you conducted a series of tests and selected samples of Britons and Frenchmen you would expect them all to give an average height near to the average for the whole population, some samples a little above average and some a little below. Rarely would you find samples which gave averages rather remote from the true average for the whole population.

In exactly this way samples of sentences give you an average length of sentence, and Wake showed that, for writers of continuous homogeneous Greek prose, all the samples from works of one author belong to one population.

Wake looked at six different works of Xenophon. The average length of sentence, for all six works together, is 18·9 words. The average length of sentence in the six works varied from 17·5 words up to 20·0 words and all the samples can be regarded as having been drawn from the one group made up by all six works. There is one work sold with the works of Xenophon called the Cynegeticus, and this one is generally agreed not to be his. The average length of sentence in this work is 15·0 words and it is unlikely that this sample could come from a group with an average of more than 16·2 words. Thus this work is significantly different from the other works of Xenophon.

This argument can be repeated for any author of Greek prose who is making up his prose and writing it down. It is, of course, a negative test; you are assuming that the works are by one author and then testing to find out if this is a probable or improbable assumption and the degree of difference you will accept as being significant varies with

26

the importance that you attach to the result. If you apply half a dozen tests to the Cynegeticus and all of them show this work to be different from the rest of Xenophon, then the overall result is very convincing. But if five of your tests showed no difference, then you would require a large margin in the other test to exclude the possibility that this one result was freakish. But the way in which this test is designed and operated means that you cannot prove that a man ever wrote anything; you can only hope to show that he did not write something. The point can be made quite clear by an everyday example. Two measurements of men's heights, one of 5 ft. and one of 6 ft. must refer to two men, but two measurements of 5 ft. 6 in. need not have been measurements of the same man. In the Pauline epistles we have assumed that Paul is the author of Galatians, and the problem is then to show how many of the other epistles can have been written by this man.

Applied to the fourteen epistles Wake's test showed that Romans, 1st and 2nd Corinthians, and Galatians were indistinguishable, with a sentence length of just over eleven words, while the remainder had much longer sentences.

In the New Testament the only criticism of Wake's work that could be made was that he had used an Oxford text of 1881 and most scholars would like to see the results based on more than one text, preferably the modern texts now available. So the first step was to repeat Wake's work in the New Testament and extend it to the standard samples which had not been covered by his study. Wake had pointed out the two limitations of sentence length testing, that you need a minimum number of sentences, around 100 for the average author, and that it will not work on dialogue. To this we have added the restriction that it does not apply to the commentaries such as those of Philo where there are a number of short sentences which are not Philo's but are quotations from the book of Genesis on which he is commenting.

Obviously work investigations of this kind are extremely laborious. You may have to count the number of words in a selection of the works of a dozen Greek authors and there will be a minimum of 100 sentences in each sample. It was for this reason that the late Professor G. H. C. Macgregor and A. Q. Morton decided to use an electronic computer to do the reading and counting. If the Greek text is typed out on a paper tape so that there is a pattern of holes punched in the tape corresponding to every letter of the text and every punctuation mark, the computer can read the text into its memory and then follow its instruction programme to operate on the text. The programme can be a simple one, asking the computer to arrange all the words alphabetically, or it can be quite complicated, asking the computer to consult a list of words which it has been given and then pick these words out from the text, counting the number in every sentence or group of, say, ten words and then drawing up all the tables needed for the statistical calculations.

When Wake counted the number of words in all these sentences of Xenophon anyone who wanted to confirm his results had to repeat the count. Anyone who wanted to know how many of the sentences contained certain words had to start from scratch. With the works of Xenophon now on tape, Wake's work can be checked in a few minutes on almost any computer and any further investigation can be added to the instruction programme.

It was to put the whole subject on a modern research footing that we consulted computer experts at the start. The next step was to consult some classicists. To them we explained our project, namely, to identify the habits which were so deeply ingrained in authors that the variations in the habits were negligible. There were technical problems, for the habits must vary from one author to another enough to enable you to distinguish one man from the other but not enough to confuse the works of one with works of another. The tests for habits must be sensitive enough to give some useful result on the size of sample which was available, about 100 sentences.

The Classical scholars then nominated a set of test

samples. They chose an author like Isocrates who wrote speeches to order and whose last epistle was completed in his ninety-eighth year; writers like Herodotus whose books run on simply; and like Thucydides who has a carefully cultivated style and an elaborate way of saying things; men like Demosthenes, who has the widest range of genre in Greek literature, and like Strabo, whose geography includes history and mythology as well as the descriptions of different lands and peoples. This list of samples is divided into three parts, the largest part, the white list, is all the genuine works of the men whose name they bear. The black list is a small selection of those works which are accepted, by the majority of scholars, as having no connection with the men whose name they bear. The third part of the list, the grey list, is a small number of works about which scholars are deeply divided. It is clear that there are some features of these works which suggest that they are genuine and others which suggest the opposite.

To be accepted, a test must cover all the men and works in the white list without rejecting any genuine work. Sometimes a test will not detect a spurious work, for authors will resemble each other in some of their habits, but this is not important compared to the fact that a test must not exclude a genuine work. Then one hopes that the test is sensitive enough to exclude the majority of the spurious works. For the reason given above, that authors resemble each other in some respects just as people rarely differ in height, weight, colour of hair and eyes and right-handedness taken altogether, so any one test might be expected to reveal many of the spurious works but not all.

When the tests are applied to the grey list, you expect them to show that some part of the work under examination, or some special feature of the work, is responsible for the conflicting impression of resemblance and of difference. Critics are divided over the authorship of Plato's 7th epistle. The analysis of the use of the word "*kai*" – roughly the English "and" – shows that the first half of this epistle is quite unlike the second half, and is not consistent with the *Apology* the other prose work of Plato. This suggests that a scholar who makes up his mind as he reads the first half of the epistle might decide against Plato, but if he had waited until the second half he might have accepted the Platonic authorship.

Though tests of this kind are simple in principle they can be quite complex in practice. Take the word "*kai*" as an example. It is an obvious word to look at; it has little connection with subject matter, for although you would use very different nouns and adjectives in writing of love and war there is no reason to suppose you would have any more or less "ands" in the one case than in the other. *Kai* is also a common word; about 5 per cent of all the Greek prose ever written is merely a repetition of this one form, and of all the Greek prose sentences written more than half contain at least one *kai*.

There are two simple questions to ask about the occurrence of *kai*: Is this word *kai* or is it any other word? and, How many *kais* are there in this sentence? To take the second question first, the investigation starts by dividing a large work into parts and testing to see that all the parts of the work are consistent with each other. Conceivably an author might use more *kais* in the first part of his work than in the last part, so that the average for the whole might be misleading. Having shown that the parts of works go together in this respect, then you must take a series of works by an author who wrote for a long time, like Isocrates in his fifty-five-year career, count the number of *kais* in all the sentences of his works and then show that the differences within the works are negligible compared to the differences between works. Only when all this preliminary investigation has been completed can you proceed to the main inquiry and count the *kais* in the sentences of perhaps a dozen authors. If all the accepted works of the authors are consistent in their use of *kai* in sentences; if the test reveals most of the spurious works; if the test is sensitive enough to give a result in the problem to which you wish to apply it, you can try it on the problem which started you on the inquiry.

Table One (at the end of the book) shows the use of *kai* in the sentences in three parts of a well-known piece of literature which nearly got into the Bible as an alternative to Revelation. All three parts are consistent.

Table Two shows the occurrence of *kai* in the works of Isocrates. There are two different ways of treating this data: one, the comparison of averages, excludes only Work 1 and the other method agrees in making a large significant difference between Work 1 and the others but also indicates a difference in Work 12, the Panathenaicus, which was not only interrupted by the last illness of Isocrates but shows signs of senility. Between the Panathenaicus and Work 2 there is a gap of fifty-five years.

Table Three shows the same data for the history of Herodotus. Again all the parts of this large work are consistent with each other. This is generally true of Greek prose authors.

Table Four shows the occurrence in the Pauline epistles. The differences between the groups of epistles are always associated in other prose writers with a difference of authorship.

The other aspect of the occurrence of *kai* seems at first sight to be simpler. All you have to do is count all the words in the work and divide them into those which are *kai* and those which are not. But there are complications. Table Two shows the occurrence of *kai* in the nine epistles of Isocrates. They are consistent in their proportion of *kai*. But if you include the other works of Isocrates you soon reach a point at which the works are not consistent. The trouble is due to the fact that the proportion of *kai* in a short work, of less than 100 sentences, is rather higher than it is in a longer work. When you examine still longer works, over 150 sentences, the proportion falls again, as seen in Table Five. This is also true for Demosthenes; the proportion of *kai* in short works, less than three thousand words, differs from the proportion in longer works, and then in the longest works it reaches a stable level. So you must take care not only to compare samples which are similar but samples drawn from works which are of much the same size. In other words, the occurrence of *kai* in fifty sentences taken from a long work is rather different from the occurrence of *kai* in fifty sentences which make up a short letter.

Another test, the proportion of sentences which have the word 'de' at the beginning, not only needs a minimum of about 100 sentences but also must be restricted to works written within twenty years of each other, for the usage drifts slowly over long periods of time. So there can never be any question of simply counting words and comparing works – the rules for sampling are quite strict and must always be respected. In certain cases attention must be paid not only to the size of the sample but the size of the work from which it comes.

The result is always the same, that some differences between samples need no more explanation than do the differences between bridge hands which are rarely identical; the chance variations of shuffling and dealing are a sufficient explanation of them all. Then there are some differences, either fairly small differences which persist over a number of samples, or large differences in single samples, which are not readily explained by chance. In the tests developed, these large differences are always associated with differences of authorship.

When these tests are applied to the Pauline epistles, after having been tried on over four hundred samples drawn from a wide range of Greek prose writers, they all give the same result, that four epistles are entirely consistent, Romans, 1st and 2nd Corinthians and Galatians. To these can be added the very short epistle to Philemon, only 335 Greek words, for there is nothing in Philemon which makes it unlikely to be by Paul. In this group there are some slight anomalies, differences which are mathematically significant but not large enough to be always associated with a difference of authorship, one is in the first chapter of Romans and another in chapters one to nine of 2nd Corinthians.

1st and 2nd Thessalonians are indistinguishable, but there are significant differences between Colossians, Philippians and Ephesians. These differences should be treated with reserve, for Ephesians is quite unlike any piece of Greek prose and may be the product of some process of literary composition quite unlike the normal methods.

1st and 2nd Timothy are also indistinguishable. Titus is so short that it is difficult to say much more than that it does not belong to the Galatians group and is nearest to 1st and 2nd Timothy.

These conclusions are important in two quite different ways. In the first place, they are introducing a measuring scale to New Testament studies, for this is a way for saying– Here are differences. Are they the differences which, in the whole class of Greek prose writers, are always associated with difference of authorship, or are they differences associated with revision or editing, or are they the differences which exist between the different works of one author and need no further explanation?

The other aspect of this work which is of consequence is that it is a new way of learning about the Bible. This may seem a simple statement and so obvious that it is hardly worth the making, but most churches take the view that although it is possible to discover some details which support the accepted positions in biblical studies, it is not possible to discover anything which will demand any radical change of attitude. The root of this belief lies in the fourth century. Many of our biblical views are still those hammered out in the disputations of that time, when, for example, the Creeds were made.

A most potent assumption made in this formative period was that all the New Testament books presented a homogeneous view of the life and work of Jesus. All differences had to be explained either as the inconsiderable variations

33

which are always present when more than one person recounts an experience or as stages in the necessary understanding of the profound personality of Jesus. Reading the Bible under these restrictions was soon a dogmatic necessity.

Now if you look at 1st Thessalonians iv: 15–18, it is quite clear that the writer attributes to Jesus the idea that the world will soon end and many of the people to whom he writes will meet Jesus coming down from heaven to earth. Against this can be set 1st Corinthians xv.: 51–8, which deals with exactly this same point. The simple idea of 1st Thessalonians has been modified and the later you go in Christian literature the further and further is the ending of the world pushed into the future. The classical explanation for this contrast is that Jesus spoke of the end of the world in a symbolic sense and that his words were, in the enthusiasm of the early church, taken rather too literally. When ardour cooled, his words were more sensibly understood and one example of the change brought about by reflection and experience can be seen in the change between Paul's words in 1st Thessalonians and in 2nd Corinthians.

But if these two views are not stages in the experience of one man but the views of two men, it means that the words of Jesus were variously interpreted by the early church. Schweitzer has dealt at length with this problem and his conclusion was that Jesus Himself expected the imminent end of the world. In other words, there is not one truth expressed in a variety of ways but there are conflicting views and the root of at least some of the conflicts lies in the words of Jesus.

Sometimes Jesus spoke of the world as about to end. The passing of time showed that the world did not end, so the words of Jesus have been interpreted as metaphorical. Schweitzer argued that this view was not consistent and that some words and actions of Jesus were only to be explained on the grounds that Jesus Himself believed that the world would end soon.

34

In other words our view of the Bible has been coloured by the preconception that any apparently contradictory statements are only different ways of looking at the same truth or different stages in the understanding of the same truth. One of the supports of this unitary view of the New Testament was the theory that the contrast between 1st and 2nd Thessalonians and the later letters is due to the passage of time and the teaching of experience. But it is now apparent that some people in the early church disagreed with Paul about the interpretation of the words of Jesus. Time may have proved them to be wrong and Paul right, but the question which still demands an answer is the question Schweitzer raised – where we have disagreed about the application of the teachings of Jesus, how can we be sure of what He actually meant?

Another aspect of this problem is the historical reconstruction of the Apostolic age. The radical German historians of the nineteenth century, headed by F. C. Baur were the first people to insist that Paul wrote only the four major epistles which this modern analysis have shown to be consistent. Baur held that one of the key issues in the formative years of the early church was a struggle between Peter and Paul, a struggle reflected in the book of Acts. This theory, however well it accords with our own experience of organisations made up of human beings, is fatal to the sentimental view of the origins of Christianity. The sentimental picture of a happy band of brothers with Peter accepted and unchallenged at their head cannot survive an analysis of history. The main issues raised by the authorship of the epistle are better dealt with after the composite books have been examined.

CHAPTER FOUR

READING THE GOSPELS

As has been said earlier, the Gospels and the other major books, Acts and Revelation, are not made up and written down by the man whose name they bear, they are compilations which he put together. Just like a biographer of the present day, the writer of a Gospel would copy into his book any saying of the man who was the subject of his book or any story which had been told about him. So you cannot take one part of his book and prove anything by comparing it with another part, for they may have quite different origins. You cannot even hope to take all the parables of Jesus and compare them with any success. The reason for this is a simple one: when Matthew and Luke both copy from the Gospel of Mark they sometimes condense the material and sometimes expand it – only rarely do they copy it exactly – and this mixed material is not suitable for testing in this way. We can see how the Gospel of Mark was altered by Matthew and by Luke because we have the Gospel of Mark before us. We cannot see how Mark altered the material which lay before him. This, of course, is saying that you are never quite sure exactly what Jesus did say on any occasion. All that it is safe to assume is that He said something like what has been recorded, though when the subject is a story like that of the prodigal son, the differences are likely to be minute. It follows that any theological argument based on the exact interpretation of a single phrase, such as the great Reformation debate about "This is my body", is an imaginative extravagance.

What you really want to know about a Gospel is where the parts of a Gospel have come from and how they were put together. Sometimes this is easy, as when the Gospel of Mark has survived to show us exactly what use was made of the material by Matthew and Luke. But without this aid progress is difficult. There is other material common to both the Gospels of Matthew and Luke which is not taken from the Gospel of Mark. The argument as to whether this is to be explained by both men copying from one account or by both copying different accounts of the same sayings or events is still going on more than a century after the discovery was made.

There is only one situation in which it is easy to spot where a source has been copied, and that is when there is an abrupt change of sense and of scene. Usually this is the consequence of the author having started to copy from some source at an appropriate point and then finding that the end of the source does not fit in with the following narrative. An example of this is clearly to be seen in the seventh chapter of the Book of Acts. The end of chapter vi reads on to vii: 55 while the section in between vii: 1–54, is a long speech which would be quite incredible in the situation. Another is the start of the twelfth chapter of the Gospel of John which begins with a note that Bethany is the place where Lazarus was raised from the dead just after a whole chapter has been devoted to this very subject.

The copying of a source is often revealed by repetition. Two of the most celebrated of these are the series of six events told by Mark in vi: 31–vii: 37 and repeated in vii: 1–26, and the dozen items recounted in Acts ii: 1–43 and iii: 1–iv: 40 which is repeated in iv: 31–v: 42.

It is now possible to test the theories of how the composite books were put together. The test depends on the fact that these books were not written on an endless supply of paper as one writes a book today, but were written to fill certain sizes of manuscript which were readily available both to write the first copy into and then to make duplicates in. With only the simplest mathematical apparatus – for example, scribes could have no idea of the average value of a variable quantity like the number of letters in a line – what had to be done was to copy from the source into the new book until some number of the columns in the new manuscript were filled by some number of columns of the source. There is no way of knowing how many columns there would be in any of the sources or any of the manuscripts, but there is no reason why a mathematical model cannot be made of them. The columns of the model might be twice the size of the original or half the size, but the proportion is preserved, and that is all that is needed to recreate the circumstances which the author of the original had to deal with.

Applied to the Gospels of Matthew and of Luke this test clarifies what many scholars have long supposed to be the process of their composition. One scholar, Streeter, argued in 1924, that the Gospel of Luke as we now have it was an enlarged version of a short book to which a new beginning had been added; some portions from the Gospel of Mark had been inserted and the ending had been revised. This theory of Streeter's fits very well into the mechanical problem of book production, which in its turn explains what Streeter never managed to explain – why the book was made in this way with so little regard for literary smoothness.

This approach enables it to be shown that Acts, the companion volume to the Gospel of Luke, was written in exactly the same way on the same principles. It also makes it possible to see how Mark built up his book and how the Gospel of John was made. These are complex situations, and each of them will in turn be the subject of a book.

In summary, the position is that we can go back one step in the creation of the Gospels and one generation in time. For example, the Gospels are usually dated by reference to the fall of Jerusalem to the Romans in A.D. 68. The Gospel of Mark has a thirteenth chapter full of warnings; when it is copied by Matthew and by Luke they change the warning to fit in with what actually happened in the siege of Jerusalem. So the argument runs that the Gospel of Mark is prior to the fall of Jerusalem and the Gospels of Matthew and Luke after it. But it is now clear that it is the second edition of these Gospels which are being dated in this way, and the versions on which the present forms are based must be earlier.

It is now easier to see some of the developments in the Gospels. Though some of the later stories, the large parables, might well go back directly to Jesus, the Christmas stories and many of the more dramatic interludes in Acts are remote in time and place from Jesus.

* * *

At this point the reader may well feel that the position so gloomily foretold in the first lines of this section has come to pass. Instead of Gospels which deal with the large and fascinating subject of Jesus they have become collections of problems. Between us and Jesus has risen a high fence of historical limitations, doctrinal influences, human fallibility and emotional unreliability. The Bible can only safely be read and expounded by experts in Greek, in Judaism, in history, in religious growth.

There is a sense in which this criticism is valid, but only the sense in which it can be said that where ignorance is bliss it is folly to be wise. These problems of understanding and interpreting the Bible exist; to pretend that they do not solves nothing.

To discover what Jesus said and did, what He claimed for Himself, and what other people claimed He meant – or even put into His mouth – is a difficult task. But so much depends upon it that one cannot avoid it.

Not only must there be careful study of the text of the Bible itself, but there must also be a continual revision of our views to take account of what is discovered in other fields than the study of biblical literature.

One old professor said, and said it sadly, that when he began to preach about 1910, the great delight of the pulpit was to expound a miracle. By the time he retired, in 1947, the miracles hung round the preacher's neck like an albatross. When he began, miracles were accepted as proof that God controlled everything and would suspend the operations of nature in favour of His people. By the end of his career science had convinced people that changing water into wine was not possible and, if possible, was pointless.

This difficulty might seem to lie outside the Bible, but this is not so. In the New Testament are stories about Jesus which, if told today, could only be interpreted as claims to be able to suspend natural laws and to perform miracles regarded by scientists as impossible. But in the first century these stories carried no such claims. The stories told about Jesus had been told about other men. In this connection the life of Apollonius of Tyana is relevant. Apollonius was supposed to be divine and his birth had been announced by an angel; he healed the sick, raised the dead, cast out demons and preached good news. He instructed disciples, warning them to count the cost before embarking on their discipleship; he was unpopular with his own family and in his own country. Finally Apollonius appeared after his death and made a speech on immortality.

The difference between Jesus and Apollonius lies not in the circumstances of their life or in the stories which record their deeds, but in their characters. Apollonius was basically self-centred and selfish. Jesus was simple and selfless. The moral principle of Jesus runs against the modern conception of His miracles – in His teaching Jesus always discouraged the idea that God had favourites or would make exceptions.

The trouble began a long time ago. The miracle stories of the Gospels are illustrations of the effect of a personality and are evidence of what men believed about this man rather than analytic accounts of what He did. The rise of science in the fifteenth and sixteenth centuries seemed to challenge the authority of the churches. But the church continued to speak of itself as above the authority of human knowledge or understanding. Geology might account for the creation of the world but the miracles of Jesus remained proof of the supremacy of God, and His chosen instruments, over all created things and rules or laws. The churches refused to countenance any natural explanation for these stories. You might point out any number of things, that drunk men have been known to praise water as wine; that men have walked out from the shore on a sandbank and looked as if walking on water; that fishermen have left a watchman on shore to point out the shoals which he can see more easily than they can; but all in vain. These stories are "proof" that God in Jesus was above all natural law and would suspend the order of nature to impress a crowd of natives none of whom had any idea that such laws existed to be suspended.

So it has come about that, in a vain attempt to erect an authority above the truth, theologians raised a spectre which they could not exorcise. What they intended to be proof of their authority became a demonstration of their credulity.

This is particularly true of some crucial issues, of which the resurrection of Jesus is the first. In ecclesiastical creeds and doctrinal schemes it is generally assumed that the corpse of Jesus was revived, emerged from the tomb, went about the world for forty days and took a formal farewell of the world before ascending into heaven.

There are passages in the New Testament which express this view of the sequence of events with simplicity and clarity. But there are other passages, notably Paul's statement in 1st Corinthians xv, which are reasonably explained as visions of a subjective nature rather than visitations from a resuscitated corpse.

In the early church the distinction between these points of view was not important. To the first century the world was flat, heaven was above your head, the age of the world was to be measured in generations, and the end of the world was a time when all the dead would rise to new life and a changed world. The problems which beset such a view, varying from the simple difficulty of providing standing room to the re-creation of a personality which continuously changes, did not exist.

But as the world grew wiser the church turned away from the challenge implicit in the growth of secular knowledge and continued to regard the resurrection of Jesus as the supreme miracle and the touchstone of faith. Since the classic expression of this event was in purely material terms, the body and the empty tomb, the churches were condemned to argue that what had happened to Jesus would happen to everyone at the last day. Some of the results of this belief were obvious. It made people think of cremation as wrong. But it had some less obvious results, such as inducing a belief that the soul entered the body at the fifth day after conception and finally left it the third day after death.

All of this, and much else, had followed from the assumption that there is one correct interpretation of the words and deeds of Jesus and that this is the one selected by the church in the fourth century.

Attempts have been made to suggest that this is providential, that God not only sent Jesus to the world but ensured that an infallible record of His life and teaching would be preserved.

By far the worst consequence of this assumption has been that whereas one might have thought that the interpretation of the New Testament could safely be left to the experts and to the churches, they are often least to be trusted having most to gain or lose by some particular interpretation.

On the Church Today

God is the ultimate authority in religion. But our knowledge of Him is necessarily partial. It is therefore easier to substitute something more comprehensible from which we can derive a precise creed and code of conduct.

The Bible served this purpose in the past, but by the beginning of this century the Old Testament could no longer bear the weight it had to carry. Not only did its history and its science belong to the times in which the documents had been written, but also its ethics and theology. No creed or code for the twentieth century could be derived from the Old Testament. Now the cruel question came up: Was the New Testament equally vulnerable?

Instead of conceding that religious authority does not reside in documents, apologists have tried to preserve their position by reinforcing the authority of the New Testament.

In the last thirty years this defence has taken two forms. The first has been characterised by the use of the word *kerygma* (message). The thesis is that not the individual documents of the New Testament but the *kerygma* of the whole New Testament is the authoritative thing.

We ignore the untidy diversities of a historical movement and concentrate on a central theme elicited from the whole corpus of the New Testament. These books, it is claimed, speak with one voice, which is *prima facie* evidence of their divine authority. This is a *non-sequitur* and also demands that a blind eye be turned to the inconvenient fact that there is diversity as well as agreement in the New Testament.

The usual method of arriving at the *kerygma* is by means of the "early" speeches of Acts. The elements abstracted from these speeches are traced out in the other books of the New Testament. Unfortunately, some books such as James, 2nd Peter, Jude and Revelation are poor material for this purpose. These also contain, as do the other books of the New Testament, additional elements which seemed important to their writers – such as the descent into Hades – which have had to be disregarded or sublimated.

This twentieth-century New Testament within the New Testament is a construct, artificially fashioned for the particular purpose of present-day apologetics. Even so, such early constituents of the *kerygma* as the second coming are not taken over *simpliciter*. When the *kerygma* of the early church has been elicited, it is still not possible to accept it as it stands. It is refined, demythologised, transmogrified.

This process has the virtue of moving in the direction of a less gross form of authority, but in fact it has the effect of prolonging the traditional idea of authority and it leans heavily on the personal authority of the first Christians and in particular of Paul, the first and indeed the only person who proclaimed the gospel in his own name in the New Testament.

Through the centuries the word of Paul has had an authority second only to that of Jesus. In some matters of great importance on which Jesus said nothing, the word of Paul has been regarded as final.

In so far as Paul's personal authority has been the main reason for accepting what he said, a number of documents are now seen to be deprived of that authority. Unknown writers can never make good this kind of loss. If, however, the documents are to be assessed on their merits without benefit of *ipse dixit*, the traditional conception of a scriptural authority is in ruins.

A second method of reinforcing the defensive position has gathered momentum in recent years. The church is increasingly regarded as the guarantor of the New Testament. The notion was rejected when the first questions about religious authority were asked by the Reformers, but is now revived in modern dress.

44

The New Testament is authoritative, we are now told, not because it is infallible or written by apostles, both these propositions having failed, but because it is the church's book, the scripture of the redeemed community. Read and interpreted as the church reads and interprets it, it is the supreme rule for faith and life.

But whoever accepts such an expedient transfers the seat of authority from New Testament to church. The interpreter has the last word. We are out of the frying-pan into the fire.

Today the following propositions are widely canvassed among church members:

1. That the church has an unchanging divine message derived from the New Testament.
2. That the church alone mediates this message as the final truth by which all are judged.
3. That the church is a divinely ordained institution with unique rights and unique authority.

This amounts to the claim that the church is the source of religious truth and that an amalgam of church and New Testament is sufficient substitute for the authority once mistakenly accorded to the Bible.

The fact that Paul's contribution to the New Testament is much smaller than theologians have believed presses home the main question of authority in its most acute form so far. In other words, we are being forced to reject finally any easy substitute for God, whether in the form of scripture or institution or both. Since the institution is increasingly regarded in our day as capable of "authorising" the scripture and so maintaining the *status quo*, we now consider the church today.

CHAPTER ONE

DEVICES AND DESIRES

The church is uncertain of its role in the twentieth century. At present it proceeds like a schoolboy whistling in the dark, not knowing how far he has to go or how long his nerve will last.

If zeal could command success the church ought to be enjoying one of its most prosperous periods. Its clergy were never more devoted; its laity never better instructed; its views have the quickest and widest distribution ever. But its direct influence on life continues to decline.

Beyond its own membership the church of today appears to meet with the least desirable kind of attitude – sheer indifference. To more and more people it is saying less and less. It would rather be persecuted or patronised; it has had wide experience of both. To count for little or nothing to the bulk of the population is new and bewildering.

It would be false to imply that the church has been utterly complacent about its failure in the twentieth century. It has become fashionable for churchmen to declare that the church must modernise itself. The Bible has been translated into more modern speech. Clergy are urged to use "the language of the people". Chaplains have been appointed to institutions and industries. Finances have been overhauled, church architecture reviewed, forms, orders and times of services altered. But the general picture is unchanged. The church appears to be exhausting itself merely to keep alive.

Concurrent with the programme of modernising, there has been a limited programme of self-examination. While the practical mind has sought salvation in up-to-date methods, the theological mind has called for a fresh

47

realisation of the nature, mission and destiny of the church itself. The past twenty-five years have seen a most vigorous inquest. Every congress and conference calls for self-examination, re-appraisal, new thinking for a new age. Never has so much been said and written about the kind of organisation the church is supposed to be and the kind of job it is supposed to be doing.

But it is not obvious that this has had any effect on the precarious situation. The rest of the world will not be impressed by an organisation in a deep mood of introspection. It must not only say what it is supposed to be; it must be what it is supposed to be. It will be known by its fruits.

Neither modernisation nor introspection can help the church in its present plight. Neither goes deep enough. Both have taken place without the church coming face to face with the real situation. For the church still believes that the crisis of the twentieth century is like all the others in its long history. It will pass and the church will go on. It does not see that it is fighting for its life. It is blinded by its traditional belief in its own permanence. The new thinking is of old thoughts.

For this reason the church's programme of modernisation has been limited to methods. It has not extended to aims. For this reason its self-examination has been directed to psychological reassurance, not to repentance.

For all its desire to meet the twentieth century on real speaking terms, the church is not prepared to ask radical questions about itself and its job in the twentieth century. It does not realise that new methods of doing the same thing are sometimes useless because it is not the same thing that requires to be done. It is unaware of the danger of self-assurance based on propositions it has refused to question. In the language of the church itself, the need is for repentance. And repentance is a change of heart, not a change of method or of self-esteem. To admit one's failures when they are patent to all the world is not repentance.

48

Repentance means saying not only, "I agree that some actions have been inadequate, mistaken, wrong"; it means saying, "I have been wrong" or even "I am wrong". It is this that has not happened.

The church, unhappily, has its own way of comforting itself when times are bad. It takes refuge in the notion that its lack of success is convincing proof of the world's hardness of heart. It speaks much of the role of suffering and of being misunderstood, of bearing the cross and dying to live, but it does not take this too literally. In short, the church is adept at doing what it condemns in poor sinners – passing the buck.

Because it has previously been able to regain some of its lost prestige, it is convinced that this will always happen and that Jerusalem will never be laid waste. What if it has run into an age which is unwilling to wait till the church gets out of the doldrums? This might be such an age, the age when the church no longer judges the world as of right but the world judges the church. A monstrous suggestion this, but it could turn out to be simple history all the same.

At the beginning of this century the church seemed to be on the point of realising that it could not talk to the modern world on the basis of authoritative claims which took their rise and had their setting in an age that was dead. It was prepared to look out on the world, see its need and ask what might be done. Now the church speaks more exclusively of itself, and the more it does so the wider yawns the gap between the church and the outsider.

In 1945, when people were beginning to think of working and planning for a new and better future for the social, political, economic and educational life of the country, an archbishops' commission produced a report entitled *Towards the Conversion of England*. The purpose was "to stimulate evangelism". It proposed new methods, but its presuppositions were more interesting than its proposals. And its presuppositions were more dogmatic than was possible a quarter-century before. They reflected the trend in all communions towards a more exalted view of the nature of the church as a divine institution endowed with authority to instruct and judge the world.

One quotation from *Towards the Conversion of England* gives us an interesting comparison. On page 17 the Report says:

> "We profoundly dissent from the assertion that there is 'an element in the (Church's) message which changes with varying conditions' . . . It is the *presentation* of the Gospel, not its *content*, that changes with succeeding generations and their varying conditions."

The statement condemned, namely that there is an element of change in the message, is from another archbishops' committee which reported in 1918 (*The Evangelistic Work of the Church*, p. 19). If the 1918 statement is an attempt to speak the truth about the need for change in the light of history, the other shows a recoil to a dogmatic position, renouncing any such attempt. Outside the church, dogmatism in this age is recognised as a substitute for real thinking.

The quotation raises the most formidable question the church has to face today. Is the church sure that it has the kind of message and the kind of authority which never changes and requires not assessment but submission? Is it a virtue in the church that it is not prepared to put this claim to the test – Has it been true? Is it true now?

It may be admitted that the church's claim to possess the unchanging truth is more sophisticated today than in the past. But it is still made and where it is not made explicitly it is certainly implied, even by those who might not be prepared to accept any overt definition of it.

The Roman Church has no inhibitions in the matter. It claims to be the one true authoritative institution, divinely appointed with a sovereign right to proclaim an unchanging and infallible message. The canons of the Vatican Council of 1870 leave no doubt. There is in the church a right and a power to assert what is to be believed and what is to be done by Christians as a matter of divine authority. How and by whom that authority is exercised is for our present purpose a secondary consideration. Whatever the mechanics of the matter, the church in relation to mankind is to be regarded as God's authoritative agency. Its truth is God's truth and by reference to its truth a man is saved or damned.

It is not, of course, to be expected that in churches outside the Roman communion the doctrine of the church's authority should find such unequivocal expression as it does here. The historical circumstances of the Reformation made this impossible.

But this does not mean that the church as an agency of the gospel was thought to have no authority to proclaim an unchanging divine message. None of the Reformers doubted that the one true gospel was committed to the church. They differed as to how the church was to be identified but not on its right and authority as a divine institution.

It is often said that the Reformers gave up one absolute authority (the church) to submit to another (the scriptures). It is truer to say that they could not conceive of the church apart from its traditional claim. Nor did they intend to make a new beginning of a new church which made no such claim. From this point of view the Reformers simply realigned the one unchanging authority traditionally believed to be vested in the church as a divine institution.

Calvin was very particular about the definition of the church, but once he has defined the church to his satisfaction that church is possessed of the traditional authority and can use the traditional language of an agency whose voice is the voice of God.

"When the preaching of the Gospel is reverently heard and the sacraments are not neglected, there for the time the face of the Church appears without deception or ambiguity."

He continues without a break:

"And no man may with impunity spurn her authority or neglect her admonitions or resist her councils or make sport of her censures, far less revolt from her or violate her unity."

(Institutes iv: 1. 10)

It is not to be wondered at that those who have been calling the church to a fervent study of the Reformers for the good of its soul are disposed to find hope of common ground with the Roman Church as they "go forward" to a new realisation of the doctrine of the church. If one is prepared to study the Reformers' teaching on the church, to believe that what they said then they would say now, to accept the principle that what was once held to be true must always be held to be true, then the logic is inevitable. Let the Romans make more of scripture and the Reformed and other denominations make more of the church and we shall soon visibly achieve the one true church holding the one unchanging doctrine.

The church today has to face the fact that two things are happening alongside each other: its claims are becoming more precious to itself; these same claims are becoming ever less acceptable to those it would convert. These two facts contain the challenge to the church's existence in the twentieth century. And time is against the church.

It is probably true that no organisation can hope to exert great influence, as the church has done, if it does not at some stage claim more for itself than it is entitled to do. There have been ages in western history which may have needed an agency exerting absolute authority if civilisation was to be spared the worst features of barbarism.

It is important to recognise, however, that each new age has its own questions to ask of any persisting organisation, and is not easily satisfied with the answers that seemed to be sufficient for a previous age. It must be disastrous for the church if it continues to be dazzled by the grandiose dream of the past, even in a modified form, particularly if it cannot produce the goods.

Today no organisation is exempt from the need to make good its right to exist. The fact that it has had a long history and has done much good will not save it. Churchmen are unwilling to recognise that this is true for the church, even if they claim that it is a divine institution. It cannot avoid the acid tests which modern times apply to all organisations, nor stave off the consequences for ever. The theory of the church is one thing, its incontrovertible history another. It is by its history and its present performance that its theory stands or falls. Its record as an organisation, whether good or evil, lies open. Can it be argued that it is exempt from any query as to whether it has been and is now what it has always claimed to be?

When Pope Paul V with the Congregation of the Index condemned Copernicus' *De Revolutionibus Orbitum Coelestium* in 1616 as "false and totally opposed to the Divine Scriptures", it seemed to be irrelevant that Copernicus had looked at the stars and churchmen had not. It no longer seemed so in 1757 when this condemnation was repealed. A supernatural claim was followed by an admission of error and it seemed to be acknowledged that Copernicus was right even if "opposed to the Divine Scriptures".

But if the church had no standing in such a matter, were there other spheres in which it was disqualified from adopting a judicial attitude? The church at that time had leisure to adjust itself to the new situation. Like any organisation similarly placed, it did no more than it was compelled to do. It gave up as little as it could. While it ceded its prerogative in mundane matters susceptible of proof by demonstration, it entrenched itself as the authority in matters of the soul. The Bishop of Rome now claimed overtly an undiminished authority – if only in matters of faith and morals.

The church in the new circumstances of the nineteenth

century appears therefore to have renounced an ancient right to prescribe the conclusions of men at large on matters in general, but to have exalted its right to prescribe on faith and morals by divine authority. For many today it is sinful to doubt that the church has this right.

If we are to deal with facts and not with theories, the story of the church is one of both good and evil. The story of its judgements, not only on matters in general but also on doctrine and morals, is one of trial and error. On such foundations, whatever measure of good has been done, whatever measure of truth displayed, no claim to supernatural wisdom and unchallengeable authority can be based.

A study of the history of doctrine gives no ground for believing that the church throughout its history has been the possessor or the custodian of final truth. This is not the role it has played, in spite of the account which the church would give of itself and the credit given to it by the faithful.

It took two and a half centuries to determine the relation between the Father and the Son. Thereafter, to believe otherwise than as the church decreed was to court damnation. But if this final truth was retrospective, what of those who lived before this decision, including the writers of the New Testament?

It took another couple of centuries to decide whether Christ had more than one nature and one will. Since correct belief was regarded as essential to salvation, why the delay?

Writing about 380, Gregory Nazianzen says: "Of our thoughtful men, some regard the Holy Spirit as an operation, some as a creature, some as God; while others are at a loss to decide, saying that Scripture determines nothing on the subject." (*Or*: 31. 5).

The incongruities of this situation have not been unnoticed. The church, it was argued, does not pronounce judgement on a matter till this becomes essential in order to rescue the truth from the toils of error. The question then becomes, Why, if the truth is in reserve, it was thought right to allow so many vicious theological wars within the church? Again, why is a period of free inquiry right before a pronouncement and sin thereafter? More often than not, the definition of a doctrine has had more to do with ecclesiastical politics than with anything else.

The church of today does not have the sanctions it once had, but does it not still proceed on the traditional assumption that somehow, somewhere and by some means it is in possession of unchanging truth? If it is not so precise about social, political and economic matters as the assumption would warrant, in matters of doctrine it remains adamant, witness its reaction to any suggestion that the Creed, the Thirty-Nine Articles, the Westminster Confession are outdated.

The following excerpt from a press letter (18.8.63) happens to have been written by a Roman Catholic, but it reflects an attitude common in many communions.

"Informed Catholics know well enough that, by definition, the Church's *doctrine* as such cannot be changed and that if they cannot accept it they have no choice but to leave the Church."

He is not complaining about this. This is how it ought to be. The church has the truth, the whole truth and nothing but the truth. Take it or leave it. The claim is not subject to historical judgement. In its own case the church reserves the right to be judge, jury and counsel for the defence. How long can the church regard this position as tenable when to everyone else it is untenable?

The church of today can be accused of perpetuating a divorce between religion and life, the division of life into secular and sacred each with its own distinct logic, and thus ultimately of reducing organised religion to a grandiose irrelevance. It has theorised itself out of the life of the people and is now making frantic but vain efforts to get back in. But how can it, if it leaves itself no alternative but to demand submission on these terms? Its evangelism

55

is bound to be suspected of being for the salvation of the church rather than for the good of men.

Until the church can convince men that this is not so, it will have no real entry into the life of today. Repentance must begin in the church's own heart. If it does not, not only will it be able to do nothing towards the conversion of nations: it will not be able to save itself.

But the real reason why the church must change is not that this is the only way to regain lost provinces. It is simply that it has been wrong in the past; a matter of truth, not of business. This must mean abandoning the kind of argument and the method of argument which it has carried over from the past in its apologetics. It must learn to enter into the world defenceless except for its zeal for the unfolding truth.

Today the churches are being flooded with propaganda in favour of ultimate unity of the church, based on the traditional conception of the church as an agency wherein dwells the final truth.

How does the church revise (but not alter) such a cardinal doctrine as that of its own nature so as to replace many churches by one church? First by finding some warrant in scripture and tradition. Texts which previously lay neglected suddenly become luminous with direction. Theologians of past ages are discovered to have taught things which neither they nor their contemporaries were aware of. The new understanding is read out of unsuspecting sources, and it seems irrelevant that it has first to be read in.

Consider the new prominence given to the words of the fourth Gospel: "that they may be one". They have become the theme song of many ecclesiastics in the last twenty-five years. It is no matter that few scholars regard these as the very words of Jesus or that they were never designed to bear the weight of ecumenical meaning now imported into them.

Consider also the assumption that if we had not been so obtuse we should have seen long ago that Augustine,

Aquinas, Luther, Calvin and Knox, to say nothing of prophets of less degree, all along believed and taught what the church in the twentieth century is now at last discovering for itself.

Scholars of other disciplines gave up this kind of bibliomancy some time ago. The church retains it because it seems essential to the church's conception of its own nature and function. What if modern medicine had to justify itself from the pages of Hippocrates and philosophy from the pages of Plato?

Such arguments in support of such a conclusion have no place in the twentieth century except in the church. They are unlikely to encourage men of today to look in this direction for spiritual leadership. Is it too late for the church to humble itself, to admit that it never had infallible wisdom and no longer needs to consecrate its own past?

If the church were to stop trying to be what it thinks it used to be but never was, it could begin to be what it might be in this changing world. But it clings to notions of infallibility which it locates now in its scriptures, now in its own constitution. They belong to the past, and the only certain thing about them is that the man of today can no more entertain them than he can entertain the idea of a geocentric universe. He rejects these ideas and also the church which cannot do without them, even if this means that he is branded as irreligious.

CHAPTER TWO

THE ROOTS OF RELIGION

Indifference to religion as it is represented by the church today raises serious questions for society and for the church. Are men now finding a worthwhile mode of life apart from the traditional hopes and inspirations of religious faith? What future has the church if it is no longer saying or doing anything that seems important to ordinary men?

That the time has now come in the evolution of the race when men can get on very well without religion is an idea which is still canvassed, particularly by some who are tempted to think of themselves as pioneers of the society of the future. This future they visualise as one in which men have at last put away childish things, including religion and its sanctions.

But the significant thing today is not that this argument is still in circulation; it is that the pristine evangelic zeal has gone out of the idea.

It was based originally on a mechanistic view of human nature, on a mistaken thesis that evolution is revelation in addition to being history, on the notion that religion is compounded of fear and superstition.

These foundations have been shaken. Who is certain today that society has no further need of the virtues associated with religious faith? Or that these could flourish if religion itself withered away?

We are being forced to ask what religion can give to society today. The further question is whether this is what the church is offering. While raucous anti-religious propaganda has diminished, is the price of religion as represented by the church too high? Are we being offered a package deal, something we need on condition we take something we don't want? Religion may have had power to conserve what is good in the past and promote what is good for the future. But does it not congeal as well as conserve and is its future only an eternity of sameness?

There is a case to answer here. All the more so since such questions are in the minds of the most thoughtful members of society, so many of whom are at present lost to the church.

Obscurantism and superstition are not hard to find in the church. Organised religion does sometimes consecrate ignorance and sanctify magic. The dead hand of the past in the shape of hallowed traditions lies heavy on the present and inhibits the future. Those who seek truth in the inward parts should admit the charge and do something about it.

But the key question is whether these defects are of the essence of religion, whether religion itself is the enemy. The humanist who cares for the values of religion in ordinary life is not so sure as he once was that they can be encouraged by rooting out religion itself. He is more inclined to distinguish between good and bad religion, to condemn the one that the other may be free to do its necessary job in society. The scientific humanist of the sixties is not less scientific but certainly more humanist than his counterpart of twenty-five years ago.

Before there could be any case for believing that religion has had its day, it would be necessary to show that men of today have not only no use for religion but no need for what religion has to give. There is little hope that the evidence could be produced.

People on the whole are not sublimely confident that science, the state, evolution, education or some other abstraction can supply their fundamental needs. There is more than a suspicion that to satisfy a man's material wants, interpret them as generously as you please, is not the same as satisfying the man himself. And it is at this point that religion has had something to say.

When a man says he is not religious, it is improbable he

means, "I am an atheist" or even, "I am an agnostic".
More often than not he is saying he is not a churchman,
though he may very well attend church on special
occasions.

He is rejecting the church but he is not proclaiming
himself insensitive to the claims and ideals of religion. He
is distinguishing between conforming to organised religion in creed and cult, and something else on which he
would set a higher value.

Precisely this is the saddest and most hopeful fact of
our time. This kind of discrimination is fateful for the
church as it is now. At the same time, in the core of it is the
evidence that men recognise the need of religion.

It is true of course that our ordinary man may be mistaken about the church. But if so, it is for the church to
convince him on this point. It is also true that there are
people in the church who are the salt of the earth. But did
the church make them what they are?

Churchmen sometimes think and behave as if religion
were a subject in the university of life which everyone
ought to take. It is taken at a college called the church and
based on a text-book called the Bible. Those who have no
degree are not necessarily wicked, but they are deprived and
their future is precarious.

This may be a travesty of the church's idea of itself, but
not of the impression it gives to the outsider. And the
impression has been created and is today maintained by
the church itself. Churchmen want to think that they have
a monopoly of religion, or at least of the only genuine
brand.

But it is as necessary to believe that there is Christianity
outside the church as that there is education outside the
educational system. It is no doubt convenient to speak of
what takes place in schools and colleges as "Education".
But we are slowly acknowledging that the *res ipsa* is much
bigger and more general. Unless religion is to be con-
stricted to mean what goes on under the aegis of an official
cultus, the same is true here.

To the non-churchgoer who differentiates between being a churchman and being religious, this is an essential conviction. The church will not convince him that it is baseless. What it ought to be doing is to support his native conviction that religion is his whole relation to his whole environment and that this is the same as the relation of his whole soul to God and his neighbour.

Religion is given in the gift of life; it is not achieved or conferred from outside. It is not mediated at second-hand like electricity from which a man can be cut off by those who control the supply; it is a first-hand experience and only he himself can excommunicate himself.

The future of religion, then, depends on the individual man's refusal to be satisfied except at the deepest level of his needs. If this leads him to detect, however vaguely, a difference between what he needs and what he thinks he is officially being offered, this is something to be welcomed. He is not therefore fleeing from God like Jonah: he is discovering, like the Psalmist, that his heart and flesh cry out for God, even the living God.

If the church will help him to interpret to himself this religious context of his life, it may not gain his allegiance but it will be serving God and man.

Now, as always, religion is a human necessity. It arises in men as God made them. We have no right to assume that there is anything in the constitution of our neighbour which allows us to believe that religion in his case is an acquired taste, rather than a fundamental need. Still less can we assume that if he is not a churchman he is irreligious.

It follows that if men were not religious by nature, no organisation could ever make them so. In theological terms, if men were not *ab initio* capable of hearing the word of God, however imperfectly, no power on earth could ever make them hear. The roots of religion are in the human soul.

This is not a romantic fancy. It does not imply that men are born good and that the proper education and environment could infallibly produce a generation of saints. It is simply an acknowledgement that religion is of God and our inevitable relation with God, and that it depends on our growing appreciation of our real environment. It is given with life or it could not be given at all: the Creator is also the Redeemer.

There is in religious awareness an area of responsibility like the responsibility of a son as he interprets and commits himself to his father's wise and good will for him. As we find God present in our life, in and over all that constitutes the environment of our life, calling for our own real and spontaneous co-operation, so we find that our decisive and responsible role is to make the life God has given us our life, all the more ours as we realise it is always His.

"Primarily Christianity, or for that matter any other religion, is a way of life, not a theological system of knowledge. If it is to fulfil its proper function in society it must be apprehended by individuals in the totality of their being, intellectually, volitionally and emotionally, so that it becomes the directive force of their lives" (E. O. James: *The Social Function of Religion*, p. 306).

This can happen when it is first-hand experience, when it has the kind of right and authority that is derived from free acquiescence in its ideals and its inspirations.

If such a conception of religion does not affirm that men are born good, it must deny that they are born evil and that the world into which they are born is under the control of Satan, by kind permission of a God who is content to let Satan have his fling till the Judgement Day.

Human sinfulness is certainly no myth. But to give more weight to it than to the creatorship of God and the providence of God is to give up looking at the facts in order to be free to develop a consistent theory. Deny that men are capable (because God made them so) of appreciating what it is to be a creature of God, dependent on the continuous providence of God, and you go on to deny that God is in any effective way in the world which men know.

If you must nevertheless believe that God is the Redeemer, you must find ways and times in which He may come back into the world He has deserted. He returns at random periods and in random guises as an alien visitor, intruding for the purpose of preventing the world from going to the devil too soon. He becomes the dark enigmatic invader, ransoming particular souls for no particular reason.

If you dishonour men more than they dishonour themselves, you degrade God, history and the creation as well. If the church does this (as it has sometimes done in the past and in some places does today) it has no message that a self-respecting man would want to hear. And more than this, it has lost the perennial message of religion at its best.

The spiritual leaders of the world have lived and taught in the firm conviction that God is inescapable always and that men are here and now capable of repentance. Humanity owes no debt to those whose teachings have been based on doctrines of total depravity, of an absentee God, of a world at the disposal of the devil.

Nature and human nature, reason and grace, all rebel against a theology which is systematic only to be ignominious. The ordinary man will have none of it, not because he is ignorant or perverse (he may be both) but because he is disposed to believe in the creatorship and grace of God, even if he cannot articulate his belief in terms of theology and philosophy.

Those who have done most to help to raise the fallen, strengthen the weak, help the sinful to make a new start, have done it on the basic assumption that God is at work in His world and men can know that this is so. They have not said that men are really devils nor have they said that men can be gods. They have conjured men to be men.

The prophets of Israel, for instance, would not be worth reading if it were not for their awareness of the immediacy of man's access to God, their certainty that God has not abandoned the world, their belief that nature and history are spheres of His activity and the hearts of men consistently either in revolt against or in accord with His own.

The beginnings of the prophetic movement are more closely integrated into the Hebrew cultus than was once thought. But the canonical prophets have something to say to humanity simply because they weren't priests and because they protested that sacrifices and ritual are no substitute for penitence. If the cultus prevents a man from doing justly, loving mercy and walking humbly with God, it is an abomination. It was in spite of their fundamental teaching that Judaism became the religion of the Temple and the Book.

We cannot ask ourselves too often how a religion which claims to spring from the life and teaching of Jesus could fail to give priority to His insight into the essential relationship between God and men. That God actively loves the world He creates, whatever it makes of itself, is a gospel. Any organisation which could regard orders and sacraments and the like as of comparable importance is retrograde.

"It is extraordinary how widely the modern world has forgotten what Christianity really is. It has to be confessed that the reproach of the situation must lie in no small part on the Church itself – or rather on those who represent the Church in the contemporary world." (John Baillie: *Invitation to Pilgrimage*, p. 12.)

No theologian should be able to persuade us that to accept his theology is more important than to trust the noblest insight of Jesus. No church, claiming to be His, ought to feel free to arrogate to itself the right to lay down conditions for communion with God which are not derived from the plain tenor of His thoughts and deeds.

"For the most part He met only the most ordinary people, but consider what He found in them and what He had to say to them." (John Oman: *Honest Religion*, p. 48).

Are the subtle and sophisticated theologies of the

64

twentieth century any kind of substitute for this? Is what the church is saying to men today as divine in its origin, as redemptive in its intention, as this? Or is this rather what men intuitively long to hear from the church, but in vain?

The basis of Jesus' appeal to men is expressed by Oman as follows:

"Jesus speaks from man to man the truth He has seen and to which His hearers cannot be blind, unless they close their eyes. He addresses Himself to the primal spiritual authority in man, the spiritual vision which discerns things spiritual. He is not as the scribes, precisely because when He failed there, He fell back on no other authority. On the contrary, He was able to exclude every other appeal except the appeal to the spiritual in man." (*Vision and Authority*, pp. 107, 108).

Such are the broad and generous principles on which what may be called the perennial theology is based. They seem too simple, too unecclesiastical, for many of the wise and prudent doctors in the church of today and of other days. For them theology is not thinking about men and their creatureliness, but fabricating a system which comprehends heaven, earth and hell, time and eternity, the essence of deity and the destiny of Satan.

If true religion is first-hand religion, it is based on the divine privilege of access to God whose providence is the greatest single fact of existence. It is the birthright of every man.

It makes nonsense of our conventional segmentation of life, our secular and sacred, the sanctity of our superstitions, our exclusive communions, our deference to mere office, even holy office, and all the idolatries which flow from the denial that One is our Master and every place is holy, even when our boots are muddy.

The religious life is the life of any man aware of his true environment. He rejoices in nature because it is not an enigma without origin. He delights in history because it is not a tale without a hero. He has no desire to be master of

65

his fate because he is content to believe that in God he lives and moves and has his being and that God is like the love that passes all understanding. When it is hard to keep faith with God, he knows that God keeps faith with him.

This is not every man's faith, but it is every man's right – and he should know it.

Meantime the church in its various denominations is absorbed in mutual congratulations at the discovery after two thousand years that all Christians should love one another and belong to the same organisation.

CHAPTER THREE

CHANGE OR DECAY

So far as the church is concerned, this decade is distinguishing itself by ringing prophecies of a good time coming. Forecasts of the dawn of a new era of unity and faith are made with increasing conviction by spokesmen of all the major denominations. It is the fashion to foresee a second Pentecost, the probability that the spirit of God is preparing some new mighty act for our day. The church is in for a great time.

This opinion is so widespread that it is bound to appear churlish to ask if there is any substantial ground for this growing sense of well-being in the church. Is there, perhaps, some sign that the percentage of Christians in the world's growing population is on the increase? Is the church's real influence on the course of life in the twentieth century noticeably more pronounced and more beneficent? Or is this new hopefulness based simply on the fact that some Christians are now polite to each other for the first time in centuries, as most of the pronouncements seem to indicate?

Anyone who stands back and looks at the situation of the church within the context of the twentieth century must be pardoned if he finds this upsurge of euphoria a little mystifying. The church is being left high and dry to cherish whatever illusions it may choose while the stream of life is changing course. That churchmen can be quite happy in a world of their own, however congenial, is set down to the account of taking religion too seriously. Either that or not taking life seriously enough.

For the church is probably the most complacent institution in the western world. Its psychological attitude towards itself and its surroundings is moribund. In nineteen centuries of history it has stored up vast reserves of confidence in its own indestructibility. Its survival in the twentieth century depends on writing off those reserves quickly and without regret, yet there is no indication that it is ready to take a comprehending look at itself in relation to the world as it really is.

Deep below the surface appearances of hectic reorganisation and readjustment, the church is untroubled by the fact that it has entered on an unprecedented era of change without any new ideas about its place and function in such an age.

Worse still, it appears to be unaware that this kind of new thinking is in any way necessary. It has every confidence that it alone can face the future with the ideas and ideals of the past – as it has done these many generations. It still thinks of itself in terms that were once more or less appropriate but are so no longer. Its attempts to break into the life of the twentieth century are vitiated by its refusal to let the past bury the past. The church, in short, is suffering from a hangover of its own history, a surfeit of smugness.

Few churchmen seem to realise that what they have been traditionally taught to think about the church may be quite unrelated to its real situation at the present time. Any suggestion that this is so is immediately countered by an apologetic, designed for other ages, which cuts no ice today and which is based on the proposition that the church has always survived because it is not like other organisations.

No institution survives automatically. And no amount of belief in its immunity from time and change can alter this fact.

But the church feels no need to reckon with this basic truth and is content to rely on its divine ordination. It believes it survives for reasons that have nothing to do with history. Its own continued existence, irrespective of the trend of life in the wide world, has become part of its sub-conscious creed.

This deeply ingrained mood of self-satisfaction demands that any attempt at reform within the church must stop short at the point where serious questions about the nature and mission of the church begin to arise. It is this same mood which dictates that, when the church is in difficulty, the thing to do is to insist more imperiously than ever on the church's divine commission as the sole means of man's salvation and that the world is being damned for refusing to listen and believe. It seems to make no difference that people are less and less disposed to accept the church on its own evaluation.

Occasionally a voice is raised inside the church to inquire with deference if it is not time for the church to consider whether it may not be mistaken. This is regarded as very daring and, of course, not to be taken literally, the hyperbolic style, exaggeration for the sake of effect.

The Bishop of Woolwich, for instance, recently wrote that "the perennial temptation of the Church is to equate itself with the Kingdom of God on earth and so regard itself as the only agent of God in the world."

Was this intended to be anything more than a theological point? Was it likely to be accepted as a trenchant thrust at the kind of delusion which incapacitates the church for really facing its own inadequacies?

If we take such a statement and use it rigorously as a means of assessing the historical truth, it is immediately obvious that the Bishop was giving us short measure. A perennial temptation is something standing over against us, near at hand and liable, occasionally, to lure us off the straight and narrow; but, thank God, we resist.

But the church has succumbed consistently for most of its history, and today there are few churchmen who have any notion of a church which is not a kingdom, if not the Kingdom of God yet certainly a kingdom, with rights, privileges, prestige and power.

It is vain to point out that the equation has no support from the New Testament, or to show that disaster resulted in those periods when the church had ability to act on this conviction. The dreams of priests and prophets and especially of those who feel called to be ecclesiastical statesmen – how their tribe has increased recently! – are more potent than theology, history and logic combined.

To all of these the church is a sacred mystery, the one true representative of God in the world, the divinely instituted organisation which continues when thrones and dominions perish. It has eulogised itself in its prayers, hymns and sermons for a thousand years and to be in the church is to believe.

Every well-established organisation runs into trouble in an era of rapid change. The church has been in trouble for some time past and the pace of change is certain to increase. The church's time-honoured formula for such an age is – a resurgence of dogmatism. But in these days this is proof of nothing but panic, the regression to the old, familiar, comforting shibboleths that served in bygone days. True, of recent years it has not been the crude fundamentalism of pre-critical days, but for all its sophistication any brand of neo-orthodoxy is a kind of funk at the future.

What, in fact, have been the reasons for the church's survival so far? They are certainly different from those in which the church itself seems to place its confidence. The ability to change, the readiness to alter its ideas as well as its vocabulary in relation to the changing needs of the time, these are the conditions a continuing organisation has to meet.

The church cannot hope to be an important and inspiring agency in the modern world unless it is prepared to face the world, to look outward at things as they are, without benefit of delusions of grandeur derived from its actual or imagined past.

This means that it must be less egocentric and more anxious to serve the needs of this generation. It cannot continue to think of itself as a supernatural agency not answerable to the conscience of mankind. It has been in danger of extinction in the past at precisely those times when it refused to move forward in thought and deed as the conscience of mankind advanced. It has survived because it finally consented to serve and was not resigned to be outdistanced by the pace of life, intellectually, morally and materially. If it had been ultimately reconciled to being the church of a particular age it would have died when that age died.

This fate readily overtakes religious institutions. They take some time to disappear altogether but they die quickly, probably more quickly than ever in this century. They are betrayed by their success. Their natural conservatism swiftly becomes a liability. The more successful they are, the more likely are they to believe they have found the secret of everlasting life. Love of the church as it is, the enemy of the church that is to be.

Through the centuries the church has had the good fortune to have bred its own reformers, who have first been reviled and afterwards venerated. Sometimes reform has come so late that it has been touch and go. Church history shows the strains of these belated adjustments. Their legacy is the massive internal problems, both doctrinal and constitutional, which are the stuff of present-day ecclesiastical politics.

What have reformers done? They have nearly always believed they were restoring the institution to an imagined pristine purity. In fact they were reshaping the organisation in spirit and in form to serve the needs of a new generation, new in its thinking, new in what it required of life and therefore new in its demands of the church. They were forcing the organisation to think of its function, to quit its litany of self-complacence, to resume its neglected service towards the men and women of that time.

The church's survival has depended as a matter of history on the coincidence of its own instinct of self-preservation and the changing needs of successive generations. It has forgotten the latter at its peril. If the two should not overlap at least to some extent, the church would then be going the way of all organisations which have died because they were no longer serviceable.

Churchmen, of course, have preferred to think otherwise and to regard the church's survival as due to its divine self-confidence. They are loath to recognise that the church's existence is so precarious. They have an ingrained belief that the church has a mysterious uniqueness which carries with it the guarantee of immortality.

But even in theological terms this thesis is not obscure. It simply means that God does not need any particular church but only the church that will serve. It means that the world does not owe any kind of church a living.

The point is a favourite one in lectures and sermons as applied to other institutions. It is the regular understanding, for instance, that the Jewish church was rejected because it failed through presumption and exclusiveness. But it seems to be believed that the terms of existence have changed as far as the Christian church is concerned. If it falls into the same state it can count on being miraculously preserved. It is more likely, however, that all the theologising in the world makes no difference here.

The sum of this is that however ancient and venerable the church as an institution may be in anybody's eyes, it exists on a knife-edge, on condition of its service to ends that are beyond its own existence. It is therefore literally a matter of life and death that it should give priority to its function rather than its status, that is, to the question whether it is a good servant of men's spiritual needs here and now. A church enamoured of its own image is ready to be fossilised.

Today the church does not command any of the sources of power. In this age of specialisation and technology it no longer has the ability to represent or to guide the varied forces that condition and sustain the life of modern men. All the evidence is that in this respect nothing can turn the clock back. For good and all the church has had to cede its direct control of one province of life after another. The good of the church itself has consequently become

72

too narrow a cause to command the total loyalty which it formerly conceived to be its due.

Unless the church is recognised as being itself the servant of a much larger and more inspiring cause which embraces the ultimate and inclusive good of humanity and all the agencies working for this great end, it is bound to become, not only in fact but by desert, simply an optional interest for people who have to live in the twentieth century.

In this respect the young churches of Africa and Asia have distinct advantages. They are unhampered by a conception of themselves derived from a bygone age in which they exercised privileged authority. They find themselves in at the birth of a new age and compelled to co-operate with the forces which are trying to make the new age worthwhile, since the alternative is stagnation and death for the church. They have no option but to be realistic and pragmatic, to consider their function rather than their status, and to conceive of their purpose in relation to the changing situation in which they are actively immersed.

Only the disposition to live in the past prevents the church in the western world from seeing that this is the actual situation in which it also is immersed. The role of the church today cannot be that which theologians and ecclesiastics have imagined it to have been in bygone history, and to continue to think and talk in these terms is to perpetuate an increasingly painful anachronism. This is what is happening as long as the delusion continues to dominate the direction of the church's efforts, as long as the language and ideas of privileged authority persist.

The church's inherited notion of the meaning and importance of orthodoxy – in creed and practice – belongs to the past but is still cherished within the church. Denominational wrangles in the present time are conducted on this basis. In many of its manifestations the ecumenical movement is motivated by the desire to reinforce the church's authority as an *ex officio* institutional power; the

73

desire for unity and understanding is good, the reasons why it is sought are suspect.

However ludicrous it sounds, the truth is that the dream of the Holy Roman Empire still haunts the waking hours of many prelates and church leaders of all denominations. Theologians are at hand who are ready to provide doctrinal ammunition for the holy war. It is hard for them to realise that in the twentieth century their dream is at best a fantasy, at worst a nightmare.

Unless the church is prepared to go on discrediting itself by trying to sustain pretensions it is not qualified to make good, it will revise its own estimate of its purpose and methods in the light of the dramatic changes which are overtaking life in this century. Both within and between the nations, a vast redistribution of the power of living is actively going on. Not only are the terms on which political and economic power are held undergoing change, but the diffusion of culture, the speed of transport, the increase of leisure, the modernisation of education, are creating new conditions of life and bringing to light new human-race problems which demand the co-operation of all agencies for good on equal terms.

The church is handicapped here by the fact that it has scarcely left behind the persecution complex which it has harboured almost from the beginning. In an age which is merely indifferent to its proprietary claims and unperturbed by its strictures, the church still reacts to the world in general in ways dictated by conditions which no longer obtain. It still regards itself as a kingdom at war with the kingdoms of this world. It remains suspicious of science, economics, education, even at times ignorantly hostile, out of sympathy with the people who are doing the world's work. It repeatedly condemns scientists for their blind ambition to lead mankind to disaster and castigates the futility and depravity of all so-called progress which does not lead men into the church's fold.

The church appears to have kept up enmity against all those agencies which have stepped in to do the jobs it was no longer fitted to do, and is eager to take credit for inspiring all good which happens outside its aegis. At one time or another it has been at daggers drawn with all the arts and sciences which have helped to make life more liveable in the twentieth century.

It is time to end this cold war, and it is for the church to move. A. N. Whitehead once wrote that:

"A system of dogmas may be the ark within which the church floats safely down the flood-tide of history. But the church will perish unless it opens its windows and lets out the dove to search for the olive branch. Sometimes even it will do well to disembark on Mount Ararat and build a new altar to the divine spirit – an altar neither in Mount Gerizim nor yet at Jerusalem."

This would appear to be a time for the olive branch and the new altar.

The place of such a church today is not in acrimonious conflict with all the creative energies of our time, nor in competition as one more pressure group contending for the bewildered soul of man. It is in co-operation with the individual man who has to live his life simultaneously as citizen, worker, learner, maker and user of tools, member of a family, child of his time, son of God.

What this modern man needs, as life becomes more complicated and challenging, is the agency that will speak for him, this particular man who is unavoidably open to change and charged not to lose his own soul.

Such a man lives between new fears and new hopes. He needs the ministry of an association not tempted to exploit him for its own ends but in honour bound to cherish and encourage the qualities of life in which he believes.

One function of true religion is to keep up the courage and keep alive the hopes of men in a perilous world. The last thing it can take part in is the spread of pessimism and panic which undermine the venturesomness of humanity. To this end the church must deepen and enlarge its concern for mankind at the expense of itself and its own flock, of its pride and its pretensions.

The Christian faith began with the ability to meet this kind of need when as yet it had no competitive power as an organisation. It can do so again and fashion an organisation to its twentieth-century purpose. The future of religion is not precarious, only the future of that kind of religion which is paralysed by a neurotic fear of change and unable to welcome new truth and new goodness unless it is first allowed to put its own imprimatur upon it.

If the church takes the place of the servant, content to inspire rather than dictate, it must say farewell to traditional rights belonging to its former status. It will make no more alliances and concordats on its own behalf. It will create no political parties. As church, it will prescribe no aims for education, institute no censorship for art, pronounce no anathemas on science. But as spirit and life it will strengthen the hands of men who do the world's work in every sphere because it believes that the world is one and God's.

It will be prepared to free itself psychologically, at whatever cost, for the kind of service that is possible to it in our day, and at the same time renew itself as an agent of God for the welfare of mankind.

CHAPTER FOUR

CREDIBLE RELIGION

In religious discussion, feelings often run high and conservative Christians exhibit a violent antipathy towards their radical colleagues. Underneath this exaggerated reaction lies a real fear, and it might seem to any conservative Christian who has read as far as this that his fear has been fully justified.

It has been argued that you cannot accept the final authority of the church, for, in addition to a natural tendency to overestimate their own importance, churches have been sometimes not only corrupt but bitterly opposed to the removal of the corruption. It has been argued that you cannot accept the final authority of the Bible, for it is a book compiled by men and women subject to the passions, prejudices and limitations of all humanity.

So what is left? Anarchy, with every man the maker of his own religion? That is the vision which frightens the conservative. Having painted the picture in these sombre colours the conservatives will appeal for a return to the loyalties and virtues of a bygone age. To them the choice is simple; agreement or anarchy.

However attractive this view may be, it can only be maintained by ignoring some fundamental facts. It forgets that a person can only believe what, in fact, he does believe. Until the day comes when heads can be opened and memories read, no one can discover what you believe unless you choose to tell him. No one can compel your assent to any doctrinal statement, though pressures can force you to mouth the words in public.

No doubt every Sunday many people stand in churches and repeat a credal statement which begins with the words "I believe", but this does not make them believe it. A little examination will soon convince you that many of them believe no such thing.

Ecclesiastics are always forgetting that you can only persuade people to believe by argument or by illustration or by example. The root of religion is personal and individual; your religion is what you yourself believe and no one else can do your believing for you.

And if religion has always begun with people, it has also progressed through people. From Abraham, through Moses, Isaiah, Jeremiah and up to Jesus, the pattern is consistent; one man's experience has become the experience of the people and changed their religion. If you argue that the individual must subordinate his experience to the judgement of the church and of the expert, religion must stay in the Stone Age. The progress of religion, like the progress of literature, art, music and all culture, is the achievement of the exceptional individual whose personal experience comes to be shared by the majority.

Yet few people, even with the remarkable record of the Bible from Abraham to Paul before them, can appreciate to what an extent their religion is the formalised experience of others. What many Protestant churches proclaim as a sign from heaven began as the personal problems and experience of Martin Luther. The Roman Church tries to invest with supernatural dignity the arguments of Thomas Aquinas. This is not stupid, for the experience of the individual, when it has been shared, does become the experience of the church; but it is unwise to forget the order of importance. The church did not create the individuals, it was the individuals who created the church. Yet the individuals could not have accomplished their work without the church. Joined in these two circular sentences is the real truth. Churches live by individuals; individuals are, or should be, served by churches.

So the great fear that religion with a relaxed authority will degenerate into the state of every man his own eccentric church reduces to the practical point that only a few people, in normal times, are really interested in the roots of religious experience. It is from this small group that advances in religious thought and experience will come.

For the ordinary Christian the social and religious organisation of the church should be adequate. If it seems to be asking too much of the churches to stop claiming that each of the 200 which exist in Britain is the one true church and to claim no more than that it is the form of Christianity best suited to its members in the twentieth century, one has only to direct the churches' attention to history. History has always dealt harshly with claims of absolute dominion.

The root of our present troubles lies far in the past, in the centuries which preceded the Renaissance. In those days the church – and most of Christendom could know only one – encompassed all of life and all of knowledge. Theology not only covered the operations of churches, it ruled the work and lives of men. Trade, commerce, industry and every communal activity of civilisation was carried on in the framework of a church which taught that the earth was the centre of the universe, and the church was the centre of the world. Outside the church was the darkness of barbarism, a potent lesson in the fruits of disobedience. Little wonder that churches grew complacent.

The Renaissance began with the discovery that many great men in ancient times, Aristotle among them, had knowledge which, if not directly contrary to the teaching of the church, was difficult to hold within the framework of the church's belief. Observation, so long secondary to theological principles, began to break out.

By the Reformation the rising tide of knowledge had become a threat to the authority of the church. No one long respects an ignoramus. With the passing years the conflict grew sharper. The creation of the world according to Genesis could not be reconciled with the creation according to geology. To the theologians the threat was very real; if the fall of man was a symbolic or allegorical story, the redemption of man by Jesus might have to be treated in the same way.

The result of this confused conflict was that the churches chose to withdraw from the world. The alternative was to abandon claims to absolute authority and eternal truth, and to live, as everyone else must, in a state of struggling to discover more truth. So the church left geology and mathematics to science and retreated into the sphere of faith and morals.

But hardly had the position been prepared than it was being eroded. Sins, once clear and inescapable, were now psychological defects for which personal responsibility was about the same as it is for short-sightedness, or were due to glandular unbalances which doctors treated on the same footing as influenza. It was the world of science which, if it did not say "to know all is to forgive all", made the law of England admit the ancient Scottish principle of diminished responsibility.

The tragic result of this foolish attempt to maintain an impossible authority is that the churches' teaching and organisation became less and less realistic. Six days shalt thou believe in the regularity of nature but on the seventh day thou shalt believe that the laws were suspended to impress some Galileans who were hardly in a position to appreciate the demonstration. Six days in the week people are to learn and to look forward; on the seventh day they must accept that there is one subject on which nothing new can be said and one can only look back.

The clearest evidence of this unfortunate cleavage is to be seen in the distinction between the sacred and the secular. People have been taught for so long that some objects are sacred that they accept without question that candles appeal to God but electric light is more suitable for factories.

It is so generally assumed – and tragically assumed – that religion is something which begins in church, is practised in its finest parts in church and is concerned with the sacraments and services of the churches, that it is now almost impossible to take any other view of religion.

Yet our religion is our life. What we do in church is only the social part of our religion and must ever be the secondary part. It is the part which is easiest to discuss and to codify, and so will always be the part most favoured by writers and teachers, but only rarely is it the first part for anyone.

The quite fantastic result of this emphasis on the ecclesiastical aspect of religion is that there are, in Britain today, men and women who live by exemplary Christian principles of love, charity, forgiveness, faith and hope, and yet feel themselves to be un-Christian because they cannot accept the platitudes of the churches. These people believe in the God whom Jesus Himself believed in but not in the God the churches have made of Him.

*   *   *

The first step towards a recovery of confidence in religion is to begin with the first principle: religion is life. God is either everywhere or He is nowhere.

Perhaps the simplest place to begin is with people's everyday life, the source of almost all the teaching of Jesus. Just as Jesus illustrated the principles of religion from the life around Him, so we must recapture the everyday life of men and women, not because it will furnish useful illustrations for sermons, but because it is the living matter of religion.

In one sense we enjoy an opportunity that Jesus never did, and our great range of life and knowledge would not have seemed to Him a burden to be borne but an endless source of illustrations of the religious basis of it all.

That life is essentially religious we may easily see from our own experience. Take, for example, the simplest fact about our life, our utter dependence on each other. Someone else bakes our bread and brings our milk, and cuts our clothes and forms our mind and supplies our words. Not only are we dependent on people who are now alive; we live because of people who lived before us. Appendicitis holds no terrors for us because it has been overcome by a company of men and women which includes such diverse figures as Hippocrates, Vesalius and Lister.

This obvious principle of dependence works in reverse. Just as we live supported by other men and women, so there are people some alive now and some yet to be born, whose lives will be poorer or richer by our life. This being so, we face the challenge – how shall we treat our fellow men?

You can say "I'm all right, Jack" and treat other people as instruments for your own purposes, but not take any trouble on their behalf. Few of the people who live by this maxim would agree that they should lie on an operating table for an hour until the surgeon has had time for a round of golf. This principle would dissolve society and leave nothing behind except an object lesson.

A common resource is to use the modified version of this principle, and treat as equals certain kinds of classes of people and regard the rest as lower beings. But whether you divide by school ties, or place of birth, or colour of skin, you never can predict who should have been cultivated at the right time, now past, to solve your problem of the present hour. The world is too complex and too swiftly changing to make this a practical guide.

The only reliable solution is to treat all men – and women – at all times and in all circumstances, as being as important to themselves as we are to ourselves. This is difficult and can be dangerous. Whatever the outcome, the principle will be a good example to others. This principle is, of course, the golden rule of Jesus.

So the everyday problem of dealing with your fellow human beings involves deep religious decisions about which you must agree or disagree with Jesus. Why you should treat people as friends and equals, even when it is much against your advantage and principles to do so, raises such questions as whether or not human beings have a right to live freely, a right above all governments and societies, a right so unqualified as to be adjudged divine.

There are many other examples of such elementary decisions in our life. There is our sense of imperfection which leads us to learning on one hand, and to a sense of having done wrong on the other. There is our perception of order in our lives and in the world and, contrasting with this order, our sense of change. These are all examples of one truth, that each of us, every day and a hundred times a day, practises his religion by making judgements of value.

We say that *King Lear* is a better book than *Peyton Place*. There is no evidence which can prove this is so and many sales figures which might suggest that this is not so. When we say something of this kind we are saying something about the kind of people who choose one above the other. This is a creative act of faith, and is one we make almost as often as we eat our daily bread.

* * *

To revitalise our religion all we need to do is to return to the world of men and to our daily life. The role of the church will then be to deepen, explain and enrich our religious life, not to control it by the measure of a bygone era. The churches were made for man and not man for the churches.

TABLE ONE

THE SHEPHERD OF HERMAS: the occurrence of *kai* in sentences

No. of Sentences having:	Part			Whole
	1	2	3	
No *kai*	68	51	57	176
One *kai*	35	42	49	126
Two *kais*	17	36	24	77
Three *kais*	15	11	15	41
Four *kais*	8	6	3	17
Five *kais*	6	1	3	10
Six *kais*	1	2	1	4
Ten *kais*	1	—	—	1
Eleven *kais*	—	1	—	1
Thirteen *kais*	1	—	—	1
Sentences	152	150	152	454
Mean *kai* per sentence	1·349	1·300	1·216	1·278
			Standard Error	0·074

TABLE ONE

The Shepherd of Hermas is a book which was in and out of the New Testament in the early years; when it was included, Revelation was often left out. The Codex Siniaticus, now in the British Museum, which is one of the oldest complete copies of the New Testament, has both Revelation and the Shepherd of Hermas in it.

The first step in establishing a stylistic indicator is to divide a work into parts and show that all the parts are consistent with each other and with the whole.

If you took 454 cards, one for each sentence in the Shepherd of Hermas, and wrote "no *kai*" on 176 of them, "one *kai*" on 126 of them and so on for all the figures of the right-hand column of Table One, and then shuffled your cards and dealt out a hand of 150 or 152 cards you find results similar to those shown by the samples of Table One. You would find differences larger than the differences between the three parts of the Shepherd of Hermas, four times out of ten trials.

In other words, the differences between the three parts need no further explanation, they are just the same kind of differences you meet in a bridge game where one hand has no aces in it but another hand has a couple.

A number of works by a variety of authors writing on a wide range of subject matter over long periods has been tested in this way and in every case the parts of the work are consistent with each other and with the whole.

TABLE TWO

ISOCRATES: the occurrence of kai

No. of sentences having:	1	2	3	4	5	6	7	8	9	10	11
					WORK						
No kais	140	59	51	72	81	92	76	77	55	57	36
One kai	41	39	53	48	63	47	42	51	57	30	38
Two kais	8	26	27	40	25	36	29	31	28	19	16
Three kais	4	8	14	18	11	13	18	23	11	11	7
Four kais	—	2	7	9	11	5	7	11	12	8	4
Five kais	—	1	2	5	3	3	5	3	5	3	—
Six kais	—	2	2	3	2	3	2	1	1	1	2
Seven kais	—	—	—	3	1	—	2	3	1	1	—
Eight kais	—	—	—	3	1	—	1	3	1	—	—
Nine kais	—	—	—	1	2	—	1	—	—	—	—
Ten kais	—	—	—	—	—	—	—	—	—	1	—
Eleven kais	—	—	—	—	—	1	—	—	1	—	—
Nineteen kais	—	—	—	1	—	—	—	—	—	—	—
No. of kais	69	140	213	309	249	222	241	268	250	171	119
No. of sentences	193	137	158	200	200	200	182	200	172	131	103

ISOCRATES: the occurrence of *kai*

No. of sentences having:	WORK									
	12	13	14	15	16	17	18	19	20	21
No kais	76	12	54	83	41	77	76	53	21	33
One kai	43	17	45	56	24	43	51	40	14	14
Two kais	33	2	10	26	15	15	15	15	6	6
Three kais	11	1	8	21	10	16	8	11	1	2
Four kais	13	—	3	5	3	5	5	5	1	2
Five kais	12	1	4	5	—	2	—	1	1	—
Six kais	4	—	—	4	2	—	—	3	1	1
Seven kais	2	—	—	—	2	—	—	—	—	—
Eight kais	4	—	—	—	—	—	—	—	—	—
Nine kais	2	—	—	—	—	—	—	—	—	—
Ten kais	—	1	—	—	—	—	—	—	—	—
Eleven kais	—	—	—	—	1	—	—	—	—	—
No. of kais	342	59	121	240	133	151	125	146	44	46
No. of sentences	200	42	124	200	98	152	155	128	45	58

87

TABLE TWO

The next step in the argument is to look at a number of works by one author. Isocrates is a good subject for an investigation of this kind for he wrote speeches to order and the subjects reflect the interests of his customers. He wrote speeches for at least fifty-five years. An argument that habits would be changed by time or subject matter can be severely tested on the works of Isocrates.

Repeating the experiment of writing out a card for each sentence of all the works, you could very readily produce differences as large as those exhibited by all but one work. No further explanation of the differences which exists between works two and twenty-one is necessary than that they are sampling differences, exactly like the differences between hands which might be dealt in a bridge game.

But the first work is generally held not to be by Isocrates and the difference between this work and the others are so large that you could expect to find them, by chance, only once if Isocrates had written not the three volumes in the Loeb Library which bear his name, but 3,000 volumes.

It is simpler to adopt the alternative explanation of these differences, that they are due to another author having written this work.

This experiment has been carried out on more than twenty Greek authors who wrote at times between 400 B.C. and A.D. 400, some were pure Greek, others were Jews or Romans who wrote in Greek. In every case all the accepted works of the authors differ from each other only by the chance differences of sampling. In all cases larger differences have been interpreted by scholars, long ago and completely independently, as being due to differences of authorship.

TABLE THREE

HERODOTUS: the occurrence of *kai*

No. of sentences having:					BOOK				
	1	2	3	4	5	6	7	8	9
No *kai*	85	73	81	79	82	78	83	80	90
One *kai*	45	49	45	48	39	48	41	48	46
Two *kais* or more	20	28	24	23	29	24	26	22	14
Number of sentences	150	150	150	150	150	150	150	150	150
Number of *kais*	96	128	106	107	116	110	108	118	80

TABLE THREE

Two successive hands dealt to you at the bridge table will differ slightly but the differences need no explanation. Just so, all these samples from the nine books of the *History* of Herodotus differ only in quite insignificant details.

TABLE FOUR

THE PAULINE CORPUS: The occurrence of *kai*

No. of sentences having:	Romans	1st Corinthians	2nd Corinthians	Galatians	Ephesians	Philippians	Colossians	1st Thessalonians	2nd Thessalonians	1st Timothy	2nd Timothy	Titus	Philemon	Hebrews
No *kai*	386	424	192	128	32	42	23	34	16	49	45	18	12	155
One *kai*	141	152	86	48	29	29	32	23	11	38	28	9	6	94
Two *kais*	34	35	28	5	19	19	17	8	9	9	11	6	3	37
More than two *kais*	17	16	13	6	17	12	9	16	5	10	4	4	1	24
No. of sentences	578	627	319	181	97	102	81	81	41	106	88	37	22	310
No. of *kais*	242	281	185	72	137	107	99	99	49	91	68	36	17	251

TABLE FIVE

The number of *kais* used in 150 sentences by Greek authors

Author	Average number of kais in 150 consecutive sentences written by this author	Maximum Variation Plus per cent	Minus per cent
Isocrates	189	24	34
Herodotus	108	22	30
Thucydides	259	17	12
Strabo	189	18	22
Xenophon	150	15	17
Plutarch	275	14	15
Aristotle	172	21	17
Plato	136	5	7
Demosthenes	186	23	28

TABLE FOUR AND TABLE FIVE

Having established the argument in two steps, by showing that parts of the same book are consistent and then that all the writings of one author are consistent with each other, i.e. that the differences need no further explanation than do the differences between one bridge hand and another, and that all the larger differences, which do need an explanation, are due to the work having been written by another hand, then the test can be applied to the fourteen epistles coupled with the name of Paul.

Table Four shows the use of *kai* in all fourteen epistles. The differences are very large indeed. In Romans, 1st and 2nd Corinthians and Galatians the writer uses about one half *kai* per sentence. The rest have more than one *kai* per sentence. To be written by the same author as the writer of Colossians, the four from Romans to Galatians would need to have had another eight hundred *kais* in them.

There are the same number of sentences in Colossians with two *kais* in them as there are in Romans which is six times longer than Colossians.

Differences of this size are only found between different authors, never in the works of one author.

It is difficult for the layman to follow an argument of this kind but Table Five is a simple illustration.

If you divide all the prose works of a variety of Greek authors into samples of 150 successive sentences, the first column of Table Four shows the average number of *kais* you would find in the samples of each author. The right-hand columns show you the maximum variation above and below the average which you will find in all his works.

From Table Four you can see that the Romans-Galatians group average sixty-nine *kais* in 150 sentence samples and the variation is just what you meet in the works of Strabo. To include Colossians or Philippians or Ephesians the range would have to go up to 150 *kais* per sample, a range of 100 per cent, three times as much as is met in the works of any Greek prose writer.